MARY EDWARD grew up in Glasgow and has never lost her affection for the city of her birth. A former teacher and educational development officer, her work in multi-cultural/anti-racist education, combined with degrees in History and Education from the University of Glasgow, engendered her interest in Glasgow's continued ability to absorb minorities from other lands and locations, and brought attention to the history of a changing community. Mary Edward now writes novels, short fiction and articles.

Who Belongs to Glasgow?

200 Years of Migration

MARY EDWARD

Luath Press Limited
EDINBURGH
www.luath.co.uk

First published 1993 by Glasgow Libraries
New revised and expanded edition 2008
Revised edition 2016
Reprinted 2017

ISBN 978-1-910745-66-3

The paper used in this book is recyclable. It is made from
low chlorine pulps produced in a low energy, low emissions manner
from renewable forests.

The publishers acknowledge the support of

towards the publication of this volume.

Printed and bound by
Bell & Bain Ltd., Glasgow

Typeset in 11pt Sabon by 3btype.com

Contents

Preface

MIGRATION AND POPULATION movements have been a feature of Scottish life since time immemorial, and the documents and text presented in this book will, it is hoped, tell at least a part of that story. Some, such as the Romans and the Vikings, came to conquer; others, in later centuries, came to settle, often driven by poverty or persecution from the lands of their birth. In the last century, also at the invitation of the British government, some came from the countries of the Commonwealth to make a needed contribution to the labour force in the years following the Second World War.

With few exceptions, the history of Glasgow has reflected these movements, as it grew from being the medieval village on the banks of the Molendinar to the industrial cesspool of the late 19th century and, not without pain, to the 'new' Glasgow of the late 20th century. And while it is true that the experience of immigrants is frequently that of intolerance, prejudice and discrimination, it would be an unwarranted distortion of that experience to suggest that it has been equal in kind, or in degree, for all groups or individuals whom chance, or plan, have brought to settle in Glasgow.

What I set out to do, therefore, was not to describe a common experience for Irish, Jewish and Asian immigrants, but rather to emphasise what has been a constant element in the life of the city, as people from diverse backgrounds have made their homes in Glasgow over the past two centuries or so. Indeed, many Glaswegians today can trace their roots to other times and other places, perhaps almost forgotten except by family name. For those Glasgow people of more recent origin, however, who for example emigrated during the post-war years from the Indian sub-continent or Hong Kong, they are now a visible minority. And, however painful to acknowledge, this fact alone can pass the experience of rejection and discrimination on to subsequent generations, to be visited upon Glasgow children born and bred.

Thus, when the first edition of this book produced, it was with a view to providing teaching material for Glasgow schools; perhaps as a point for starting some children towards recognising their own identity, and developing a more informed understanding of others among whom they live, or, in their adulthood, may work alongside. The material is, and will continue to be, used in the classroom, but the rich deposits of the history of Glasgow's population have barely been mined by my efforts, and if the wider publication of this selection encourages further and deeper study by others then it will have served a useful purpose.

In support of the original manuscript for publication to Glasgow City Libraries I must thank Glasgow Division, formerly of Strathclyde Region Education, since it was as a teacher belonging to that authority through which I was encouraged and supported in researching and writing this text; particularly by Keir Bloomer, the then Education Officer, and Philip Drake, Divisional Education Officer.

For material and assistance with this book I have a great many people to thank who have given generously of their time, interest and their own work, and I trust that my gratitude will be apparent in the revised acknowledgements.

Finally, may I emphasise that *Who Belongs to Glasgow?* does not aspire to be a definitive or exhaustive account of such a long and vibrant period in the history of the city. Moreover, in this revised edition, it will be apparent that trying to capture the constantly changing demographic of the city in a single portrait must be likened to pushing water uphill – the words no sooner committed to paper than the events they describe are moving on. (For example, more than 100 first languages are spoken by pupils in Glasgow's schools at the present time.) And it remains to say that while many people helped and encouraged me in this new edition – particularly Gavin MacDougall, Director of Luath Press – if there are errors in the text presented then these are mine alone.

Mary Edward
Glasgow, November 2016

Foreword

THE TITLE OF Mary Edward's admirable book is *Who Belongs to Glasgow?*. In it, she seeks to answer the question with a comprehensive account of the backgrounds of the people of our wonderful city. As the direct descendant of Irish immigrants, I am personally aware of, and of course proud of, the way in which my family background reflects this rich diversity.

Mary Edward's new edition is notable in that it includes accounts of the two most recent sets of new Glaswegians: those people who have chosen to come to Glasgow to work from Poland and the other new Member States of the European Union; and the many asylum seekers and refugees who have arrived from a wide range of troubled countries. In the case of asylum seekers, in particular, it cannot be claimed that every arrival leads to a happy outcome. But I hope for a time when every person arrives they will know that they are welcome in Glasgow; to live here, to work here, to educate their children here.

Our city provided the opportunities and the means to succeed to my grandparents and to all of the new arrivals from the communities so well set out in this book. I look forward to a position whereby I can be proud that we continue to do so into the 21st century. After all, when we are asked the question 'who belongs to Glasgow?', the answer is already: 'the world belongs to Glasgow'.

In informing us so well about ourselves as Glaswegians, this book provides a vital service. I would commend it to all who are interested in their own past and predecessors, and even more so to those who wish to know more about those of their neighbour and their fellow citizen.

Rt Hon Liz Cameron
Former Lord Provost of Glasgow (2002–7)

Acknowledgements

THANKS ARE DUE to the following for assistance in provision of materials and for kind permission to use documents, photographs or illustrations.

The proprietor of the Amber Restaurant; the proprietor of Asha Fabrics; *Daily Record*; *The Herald*; *The Glaswegian*; *Evening Times*; Hong Kong Government Office; Ezra Golombok, proprietor of *The Jewish Echo*; the proprietor of the Koh I Noor restaurant; *New Statesman and Society*; the proprietor of the Oriental Pak; People's Palace, Elspeth King; San Jai Project; *Scottish Field*; *Scottish Geographical*; Scottish Immigrant Labour Council; *A Scottish Shtetl*; Strathclyde Community Relations Council; A & C Black, publishers of *The Phoenix Bird Takeaway*, by Karin Mackinnon, with photographs by Jeremy Finlay; Glasgow University Library Special Collections; the proprietor of the Sun Restaurant.

J. Singh Bedi, Wladyslaw Bednarek, Diane Edward, Harvey Kaplan, Leon Koczy, Bashir Maan, Gurmeet Mattu, Chai Ken Pen, James McArthur, Karin McKinnon, B. Saggu, Tania Sannino, Martin Shields, Ellis Sopher and Alma Woolfson.

In addition, I would like to thank Alison Grey of SRC Archives, the staff of the Glasgow Room, the Mitchell Library; and for typing the original manuscript, Alice Pickering, Glasgow Division Education.

Additional thanks must go to the following: Hilary Bell, Luath Press; David Cameron, photographer; Pat Malcolm, Clydebank Central Library; Boyd Robertson, Reader in Gaelic Education, Strathclyde University; Rona Macdonald, Gaelic Arts Development Officer; Tom Main, Tir Connaill Harps; Tony Cimmino, O Sole Mio Restaurant; Harvey Kaplan; Fiona Frank; Sharon Mail; Paul Harris, Editor, *Jewish Telegraph*; Leandro Franchi and Massimo Franchi of Franchi Finnieston; Bartek Korzeniowski, Polish Taste; Mohammed Sarwar MP – Consituency Office; Finola Scott; Robert Perry (photographer) and *Scotsman* Newspapers; Liam Stewart and Catrin Evans – Village Story Telling Centre; and Jason Bergen, Oxfam; Office of Humza Yousaf MSP.

Introduction

GLASGOW IS A 'multicultural' city: a home to many cultures. To speak of 'cultures' in this sense is simply to use one word to suggest the diversity in ethnic origins, language, customs or religion that is found among the population of present-day Glasgow. The diversity is not new; Glasgow also has a multicultural past. For almost 200 years the population of Glasgow has comprised people from other parts of Britain or further afield. Many are the descendants of people who came to Glasgow from the Highlands or from Ireland in the 18th and 19th centuries; today, many are the children or grandchildren of people who came from other European countries or who have come from India, Pakistan or Hong Kong. Or more recently, as asylum seekers or migrants from the European Union. Now they are all Glaswegians – the people who, in the words of the famous song, 'belong to Glasgow'.

Long before it was possible to 'belong to Glasgow', however, when the city did not yet exist, the population of Scotland was already of mixed origins. No less than five distinct ethnic groups occupied or invaded what was then North Britain in the centuries after the Roman occupation. These different peoples were Picts, Britons and Angles, and a tribe called the Scotti, who invaded from Ireland in the 5th century AD. The last, at the end of the 8th century, were Scandinavians occupying much of the north and west of the country. For several centuries, 'Scotland' consisted of these groups, each occupying a distinct territory and each with their own language and traditions. Only gradually did these groups come together in some loose allegiance to the kings of a united Scotland.

Following the Norman Conquest of England in 1066, Norman influence reached Scotland, particularly during the reign of David I. Norman ways in law, civil administration and in the development of burghs, together with common worship in the Western Christian church, also helped, in time, to dissolve the distinctions between Angle, Pict and Briton. (Robert Bruce, one of Scotland's most famous kings, was of Norman origin, and names such as Bruce or Sinclair remain today to remind us of this Norman element in the Scottish people.) Thus, the Lowland Scots gradually emerged, a people eventually speaking a common language. Partly because of the geography of Scotland and the difficulty of communications, the northern and north-western parts of the country retained a separate identity in the person of the Highlander, with his Gaelic language and culture.

In later centuries, moreover, the frequency of wars between Scotland and England also had a part to play in reducing earlier differences and drawing Lowland Scots closer together towards a common identity. The English and Scottish crowns united in 1603, followed by the Union of Parliaments in 1707. Scotland was, by this time, the country that we recognise today, with Edinburgh as its capital – but what was happening to Glasgow?

The small village of Glasgow – believed to have been founded in the year 550AD by her patron, St Mungo – became a 'city' when the cathedral was raised on the site of St Mungo's wooden church. Between 1175 and 1178 Glasgow also became a burgh and began to develop as a market town, but it was as a church centre that the town would grow in importance, progressing steadily until it was the city described by Daniel Defoe when he visited in 1727:

> Glasgow is a city of business, and has the face of foreign as well as domestick trade; nay, I may say, 'tis the only city in Scotland, at this time, that apparently increases in both. The union has, indeed, answered its end to them, more than to any other part of the kingdom, their trade being new formed by it; for as the union opened the door to the Scots into our American colonies, the Glasgow merchants presently embraced the opportunity; and though, at its first concerting, the rabble of this city made a formidable attempt to prevent it, yet afterwards, they knew better, when they found the great increase of their trade by it; for they now send near 50 sail of ships every year to Virginia, New-England and other English colonies in America.

It was after the Union of 1707 that Glasgow really began to 'flourish' as a centre of trade and commerce, and the 18th century saw the transformation of Glasgow from a small town of 12,000 inhabitants into a rising industrial city. As Defoe noted, the Union was unpopular at first but it brought a new prosperity to the city by enabling her merchants to trade with England's territories in America. Glasgow ships were soon sailing to America with manufactured goods and were bringing back raw materials such as sugar, tobacco leaf and, later, cotton.

Glasgow was growing in prosperity and in population: when the first official census took place in 1801 the population had risen to 77,000, but only 100 years later the figure was ten times greater, and Glasgow had a population of three-quarters of a million! Some of this growth was due to surrounding districts, such as the Gorbals and Anderston, becoming part of the city, but much more of the dramatic rise in population was the result of people coming from other places, seeking to earn their living in the industrial city and often driven by poverty, hunger or persecution from the land of their birth.

Glasgow continues to attract people from other parts of the world, and many nationalities are found in the city, including those who came in the later decades of the 20th century from countries as diverse as Chile and Vietnam.

The 21st century, however, has dawned to the accompaniment of significant migrations from Europe and many countries further afield. The expansion of the European Union to 25 countries in 2004 has opened the doors of the United Kingdom to migrants from former eastern bloc countries such as Lithuania, Ukraine, and, in particular, Poland. For the most part, these migrants are young people looking to advance in education or employment. Many will return to their home countries, but many will choose to remain, thus alleviating, to some extent, the declining population of Scotland.

Less happy, perhaps, are those who find themselves in the city as asylum seekers or refugees. Glasgow City Council, to date, is the only local authority outside London to have accepted asylum seekers under dispersal arrangements, which have been in place since 2000. Many of the immigrants of the last two centuries are the subject of this book – men, women and children who have fled their own country in search of the freedom to live without fear. At no time has this been more poignant than in the Spring of 2016, when a massive crisis of refugee and migrant movements from the Middle East is currently taking place. (See Chapter 10)

The Scottish Government, mindful of the need to promote a harmonious society, conducts the campaign 'One Scotland: No Place for Racism'. The campaign is designed, amongst other things, to raise awareness of racist attitudes and recognise the valuable contributions that other cultures have made to our society, and in effect looks to 'a Scotland at ease with its diversity' (Malcolm Chisholm, Minister for Communities, 2004).

More recently the Scottish Government has committed itself to an extensive new approach in the 'Race Equality Framework for Scotland – 2016–2030.' Working in partnership with a number of organisations this policy was launched in March 2016.

In an age of instant and all pervasive social media, which can be a powerful force of racial harassment and bullying, particularly for vulnerable young people, no formal or informal organisation can afford to conduct its affairs in ignorance of these important issues. It is to be hoped therefore, that this revised edition of *Who Belongs to Glasgow?*, by making a further contribution to the literature of migration, also serves to generate a better understanding of our multicultural society.

CHAPTER I

Glasgow and Slavery

BY THE EARLY 19th century, Glasgow people were proud of their city and the way in which it had grown from a small village. By this time, there were a number of rich Glasgow merchants who were the owners of thriving export and import businesses, and who built grand establishments in the city to demonstrate their new wealth. Known as the 'Tobacco Lords', these men had captured more than half of the tobacco trade on the other side of the Atlantic and they paid for the tobacco imported by sending over all kinds of manufactured goods.

Several Glaswegians wrote histories of the city that tell us much about these wealthy merchants and the streets that bear their names, such as Glassford Street, or the names of the places with which they were associated, such as Virginia Street and Jamaica Street. The histories also give detailed information about the types of goods sent, the quantities and their value; but something they almost never mention is that much of the wealth of these Glasgow merchants was made from trading, not only in sugar and tobacco but also in human beings – slaves from the west coast of Africa. One writer described it as 'a magic money machine', as slaves were shipped out to America and the West Indies to work the plantations which sent back the tobacco, sugar and cotton for Glasgow's manufacturing industry. It has been estimated that Britain's slave merchants (in Bristol, Liverpool and Cardiff, as well as Glasgow) netted a profit of about £12 million on the two million Africans they bought and sold between 1630 and 1807, the year in which the British trade in slaves was stopped by an Act of Parliament.

Because most of the Glasgow histories were written after the abolition of the slave trade, the writers do not mention Glasgow's part in this shameful 'Triangular Trade' as it was called. One modern Glasgow writer, Jack House, is much more frank, and has said that the Glasgow Tobacco Lords were among 'the biggest slave traders in Britain'. Slaves were not known to have been marketed in Glasgow as such, in the way that they were in Liverpool or Bristol, but there is plenty of evidence to show that Glasgow did have fairly strong connections with slavery in the late 18th and early 19th centuries.

Earlier, there is known to have been a small black community centred on the King's court as far back as 1500. In 1505 the records show payment for 'Moors' included in other cargo from Portugal, where trading in blacks was common, and in 1513 the King authorised a New Year's gift to 'the twa blak ladeis'. Glasgow's connection with black people came later, however. There is, for example, the evidence of one William Colhoun, who wrote a number of letters to his sister, Miss Betty Colhoun, who lived 'opposite the New Wynd, Trongate, Glasgow'. One of his letters, written from Senegal in West Africa in July 1770, tells his sister about his first experiences aboard a slave trader:

> We shall sail tomorrow with a hundred and 50 slaves for Potuchan River in Virginia in a very fine vessel which I am chief mate of... it is a very precious cargo as for me it is the first time... plenty of noise and stink.

William's next letter, dated October 1770, tells Betty that the slaves were sold in Maryland in America and that the ship is returning loaded with tobacco. Over the next few years, William made several voyages with the slave traders, and kept in touch with his sister Betty, who, in the meantime, after writing to William for advice, married a Glasgow merchant, Mr Archibald Peterson. After this, William wrote to his new brother-in-law about his dealings in slaves.

Writing from Sierra Leone in April 1775, William wanted to find someone who he could trust to deliver 'three prime slaves':

> Let me hear your opinion in this affair and I will remit three prime slaves which will amount to 120 pounds sterling.

If this transaction is successful, William intends to take 'every opportunity' to lay up some funds for his eventual return to Glasgow. Captains, ships' mates, surgeons and other officers were allowed a few 'privilege negroes' [sic] from the cargo as a kind of bonus for their services in addition to their wages, and William Colhoun was putting his profits in the bank to save for his future. At the same time, he would use some of the money to buy the most ordinary things. He wrote to Peterson to ask him to send some shoe brushes and polish, thread for shirts, and some new jackets and trousers:

> I have sent likewise by Captain Richard Wilding of Liverpool two fine slaves to be sold at the West Indies and the money or

bills to be remitted to you, which out of the first part you will pay yourself what I owe you and likewise pay for those things that I require. The slaves will come to about 80 pounds sterling – and put the rest in the bank.

The purchase of domestic trifles from the sale of human beings is callous and inhumane to modern opinion. To the 18th-century slave merchants, however, black Africans were in fact regarded as objects, to be valued only in terms of profit or loss.

Nonetheless, not all of William Colhoun's slaves were to be sold:

Sir, I have a very fine girl about 12 years of age. I have had her 18 months with me. She is very smart and will learn anything that is shown her. I have a great regard for the girl and I don't mean to sell her if my sister Betty will accept her I shall send her home, she can speak good English and I was the first white man she ever saw. If Betty will not have her you may ask Janet if she will be of any service to her and she shall have her. If not I know not what to do with her as I never shall sell her. She has been more service to me than any white woman that I ever knew except Mother. If it please God to spare me my life for two or three years until I come home she will be more careful over me in my old age than any white I can get.

Some things in this letter suggest that William Colhoun had treated this particular slave with a certain degree of humanity and had taught her to speak English. But she was a slave and his property, and so he was free to dispose of her in any way he wished. He is proposing to give the black girl to his sister as if she were a toy or a puppy. Slaves were not regarded as having the same kind of human feelings as white people, and so it seemed perfectly acceptable to Colhoun that this girl should have been taken from her parents when she was only 10 years old to be sold to the first white man she had ever seen. However kindly he refers to the girl, she does not seem to have a name; and if she does, William Colhoun will not use it in a letter to his family.

William Colhoun's letters end around 1776, so we do not know if the young black girl ever came to Glasgow. We do know of several others who did live in or around Glasgow as the human 'property' of their masters. We also know that these domestic slaves frequently tried to escape. It was

Letter by William Colhoun dated 6 April 1776. He writes to his brother that he has given to Captain Richard Wilding 'two prime slaves which he was to dispose of in Jamaica and he was to remit the Value in a Bill to you'.

commonplace to see advertisements (see p.6) searching for runaway slaves in the newspapers of the day.

Some rich people liked to have black slaves, who they would dress up in fancy livery, and it became something of a status symbol to have a servant whom you had actually bought. Many of these were children, like William's servant girl, and if it had not been for the powerful anti-slavery movement, we would have been able to see how one Glasgow master dressed his black slave. The *Glassford Portrait*, which can be found in the People's Palace in Glasgow, is a very large painting and depicts prominent merchant John Glassford with his wife and children at some time around 1767. The picture was painted at their home, the magnificent Shawfield Mansion in Trongate, which was demolished in 1792 to make way for Glassford Street. If the painting is examined closely it is just possible to make out, behind John Glassford's chair, that there has been another person portrayed. This was the figure of the Glassford black slave, which is believed to have been removed from the painting when the anti-slavery movement was at its height in Glasgow.

By the end of the 18th century, the belief that slavery was an evil practice was ever growing, but there are records of a few of the slaves who came to Scotland. One of these was Joseph Knight, who had been bought from a cargo of slaves put on sale in Jamaica. A Mr John Wedderburn bought the boy, then aged about 13 years old, around 1766, and gave him the name Joseph Knight, thus obliterating his African name for all time. Mr Wedderburn took Joseph into his family and trained him to be his personal servant, providing him with some education. Around 1771, Joseph was brought to Scotland and baptised a Christian. Some time later, Joseph, having been taught to read, put his education to good use. Having read of a case in England, in which a black slave called Somerset had gone to the House of Lords in an attempt to be declared a free man, Joseph concluded that he himself was now free and declared his

In this portrait of the Glassford family, the black slave would have been seen standing behind the members of the family seated on the left of the group.

Reproduced by kind permission of the People's Palace, Glasgow.

intention to leave his master. Mr Wedderburn took Joseph to the Justices of the Peace in Glasgow, who ruled that Joseph was not free to leave his master. Joseph went to the Sheriff Court and finally the Court of Session, where it was declared after a long debate that Joseph was a free man:

> Whether a British subject having acquired the property of a negro [sic], under the authority of British statutes, shall lose the property by the mere circumstances of his bringing the said negro to Scotland.

The anti-slavery movement, which fought against the practice of buying and selling human beings for profit, also fought against the conditions in which slaves were kept at home and abroad. Slaves were often beaten, kept in appalling living quarters and shackled with chains if they tried to run away, which many of them, quite naturally, tried to do. In

DESERTED,

FROM his Maſter's houſe in Glaſgow, on the morning of Saturday the 3d current,

A NEGRO MAN.

He is about 35 years of age, and 5 feet 9 or 10 inches high, pretty broad and ſtout made, broad faced, and ſomewhat yellowiſh complexioned. The white of his eyes are remarkably tinged with black, and he has a ſurly gloomy aſpect His dreſs when he ran off, was an olive coloured thickſet coat, jacket and breeches, a black wig tied behind, and ſilver buckles in his ſhoes ; but as they were all good, it is probable he would change them for worſe, and thereby ſupply himſelf with caſh.

His name is THOM, but ſometimes he aſſumes the name of THOMAS DIDDY.

A Reward of FIVE GUINEAS, and payment of all reaſonable charges, is hereby offered to ſecure the ſaid Negro in any jail in Scotland, ſo as he may be kept ſafe, and delivered to his Maſter's order. The money to be paid by Mr John Alſton merchant in Glaſgow, upon notice being ſent to him of the Negro's being ſecured.

All ſhipmaſters are hereby cautioned againſt carrying the ſaid Negro abroad ; and if any perſon harbours him, or aſſiſts him in making his eſcape, they will be proſecute therefor.

Advertisements like this would not have been uncommon in Glasgow newspapers in the 18th century.

1807 trading in slaves was abolished in Britain by law: this may have put an end to the buying and selling of slaves, but it did not free those who were already enslaved on the plantations of the West Indies and America.

In any case, it is apparent that owning slaves who were well out of sight on the other side of the world troubled the conscience less. One Glasgow merchant, J. Cunningham of 'Craigend', now the name of a housing estate in the East End of Glasgow, owned a sugar plantation in Jamaica worked by slave labour. In May 1812, Cunningham wrote to his plantation manager, a man called Taylor Cathcart:

Edin^g
29th May 1812

Dear Taylor

I have had the pleasure of receiving yours accompanied by a list of negroes and stock on Grandvale – I am happy to observe that the increase in births is likely to keep pace with the decrease occasioned by the deaths of the old and infirm people and I am so pleased to see that you afford every comfort to the women in a state of pregnancy. Indeed, I suppose you will always be disposed to do everything in your power for the comfort of all the slaves. It will be a very satisfactory and consolatory reflection to you after you have relinquished the management and retired from that situation in life.

It is clear that Cunningham did not wish his manager to suffer from residual guilt about the treatment of the slaves in his charge once he had left that occupation and returned to Glasgow. It does express some kind of concern for the slaves, but less than is shown further in the letter when he refers to one of his own children being unwell. Cunningham also writes in a casual way about Cathcart's family and so on; like William Colhoun's 'shopping list', there is no indication that it might be, at the least, insensitive to discuss domestic trivia in the same letter that concerns his human property. The slaves, after all, were a simple part of the 'machinery' of the plantation business.

Cunningham does not appear to have been the worst of slave owners, nor Cathcart the worst of overseers – many of whom were brutal almost beyond description.

The Anti-Slavery Committee had branches throughout the United Kingdom, including Glasgow. In 1823, it circulated a publication which stated that:

> In the Colonies of Great Britain there are at this moment upwards of 800,000 human beings in a state of degrading personal slavery.
>
> These unhappy persons, whether young or old, male or female, are the absolute property of their master, who may sell or transfer them at his pleasure, and who may also regulate according to his discretion (within certain limits) the measure of their labour, their food, and their punishment.
>
> Many of the slaves are (and all may be) branded, by means of a hot iron, on the shoulder or other conspicuous part of the body, with the initials of their master's name, and thus bear about them, indelible characters, the proof of their debased and servile state.
>
> The Slaves, whether male or female, are driven to hard labour by the impulse of the cart-whip, for the sole benefit of their owners, from whom they receive no wages; and this labour is continued, (with certain intermissions for breakfast and dinner) from morning to night, throughout the year.

It was not until 1838 that the movement's aims were achieved, when an Act of Parliament abolished slavery throughout the British Empire.

Following abolition, a number of black people began to come to Britain to fight for the abolition of slavery in America. The American colonies had been lost in the American War of Independence between 1775 and 1783. Some of those who came were free men but others were slaves who had run away from their owners in America. A small group of these people made their home in Glasgow between 1830 and 1860: these were, for the most part, articulate, well-educated people, who fought for their cause from their base in Glasgow and took part in the Glasgow Emancipation Society. Among these people were William and Ellen Croft (Ellen was light skinned and the couple made their escape from America with her husband posing as her black servant); Sarah Redmond, a black sculptress; William Wells Brown, a literary man; and James McCune Smith. James was born free and educated in New York City in the African Free Schools. A talented young man, James was refused entry to American medical schools because he was black. He came to Scotland and was accepted by Glasgow University, where he gained the degrees

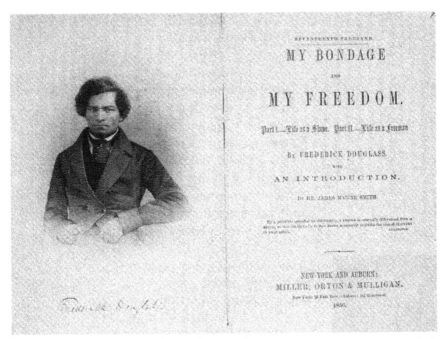

James McCune Smith, who wrote the introduction to this autobiography, was a black American who graduated as a doctor of medicine from Glasgow University.

of BA (1835), MA (1836) and Doctor of Medicine (1837). Dr Smith later returned to America and was active in movements for the abolition of slavery and the improvement of conditions for free blacks, as was Frederick Douglass, perhaps the most famous of runaway slaves.

Frederick Douglass also came to Glasgow and purchased his freedom from slavery with the help he received here. Between 1845 and 1847 he travelled all over the country, lecturing and raising public opinion on the fight for the abolition of American slavery. On his return to America, he was to publish his autobiography in 1855, with an introduction written by Dr James McCune Smith.

Just after Douglass returned to America, another man, whose experience had been that of the slave ship and the marketplace, died in a quiet little village in Dumbartonshire. His grave stone is there in the village churchyard of Rosneath, carefully tended and kept clean so that the inscription is easily read. Robert Story was in fact owned by Robert Storey, who gave him both his name and his freedom, though he remained his servant.

IN MEMORY OF
ROBERT STORY,
a native of Western Africa
In early life
torn from home & sold in
Rio de Janeiro as a slave:
there for his good fidelity
he was set free by his master.
Whom loving
he followed to this Country
and who retains the most
grateful remembrance of his
faithful services.
In this Parish
He dwelt for many years,
an example to all servants for
honesty, sobriety and truthfulness.
Ever reverent to his superiors,
obliging to his equals,
kind and courteous to all
his most blameless life
after every suffering meekly endured
through faith in a Redeemer's love
was closed in peace and hope
in the thirtieth year of his age
on 4th day of August
1848.

Most of the people who emigrated to Britain from the West Indies after the Second World War landed at ports in the South of England. Many of them were heading for London and jobs with London Transport, who had asked them to come and fill the desperate labour shortages created by the war. Likewise, the industrial cities of the Midlands were crying out for labour, as was the newly formed National Health Service. The jobs filled by the immigrants were often those with low wages and long, unsocial hours, which the post-war population of Britain did not want, since there were plenty of other jobs to choose from.

As British citizens, moreover, thousands of West Indians had served in the war, and many of them had spent time in this country, so that when recruiting schemes were set up in Barbados and Jamaica to bring workers to Britain there was a ready response. These people were British citizens who, as there is much evidence to suggest, regarded Britain as the 'mother country'. There is now a whole generation of the children of West Indian parents who have been born here. This new generation is not West Indian, but British, just as the children or grandchildren of other immigrant groups who have settled in this country since the Second World War are also British, and sometimes Scottish, or even Glaswegian.

In the census of April 2001 around 2,000 people identified themselves as African or Caribbean in Greater Glasgow, but it was suggested in 2005 that the figure was closer to 3,000.

The gravestone of Robert Story in Rosneath churchyard.

However, by 2007 the World Development Movement estimated that there were around 13,000 Africans from at least 25 countries living in Scotland, the vast majority of whom were to be found in Glasgow. By the

time of the 2011 Census for Glasgow, however, there had been a significant increase in residents describing themselves as Black, African or Caribbean to the point where they accounted for some 20 per cent of the black and ethnic minority population in the city.

Amongst that number we may find Jackie Kay, much lauded poet and novelist who in 2016 was appointed Scotland's Makar. Jackie, born in Edinburgh, is the daughter of a Scottish mother and a Nigerian father. Although a happy and secure child of adoptive parents, even growing up in Bishopbriggs Jackie sometimes had to run the gauntlet of insensitive comments about her identity.

Jackie Kay.
Photograph by Denise Else

Others of that number consists of students from African countries attending the city's universities and colleges, but a significant group is asylum seekers. At the time of the G8 summit in July 2005, when the world's richest nations gathered in Perthshire, a report in the *Evening Times* highlighted the distressing circumstances of some of the Africans living in Glasgow.

Khadija Coll, a Somalian, former *Evening Times* Scotswoman of the Year finalist and the then Development Officer for the African and Caribbean network, spoke of the experiences of African refugees and asylum seekers who were struggling to make a new life in the city in the face of poverty, fear and racism:

> People who may have been teachers, doctors or nurses in their home countries become demoralised while seeking asylum and barred from working.
>
> *Evening Times*, 2 July 2005

This included people like Able Miller, a former opposition MP in his home country of Zimbabwe. Able, who was granted asylum in 2001, had escaped torture and possible death in his own country, only to find himself living in fear for his wife and children in Glasgow as they became the targets of vandalism and racist abuse.

Maurice Kaxoka, originally from Zambia, came to Glasgow as a student. In 2005 he was working with Strathclyde Police on a range of anti-racism initiatives. He said, 'A lot is being done to tackle racism, but we need to work together.'

Working together is a guiding principle of many organisations concerned with the welfare and development of the various minority ethnic communities in Glasgow and beyond. Amongst these is BEMIS, the national ethnic minority led umbrella body supporting the development of the ethnic minority voluntary sector in Scotland.

> Another is the The African and Caribbean Network, whose mission statement strives to promote the inclusion of African and Caribbean residents as equal and valued members of the community, alleviate and eradicate discrimination through raising awareness of the issues, facilitating a joint working approach, influencing policy and provision at all levels and empowering African and Caribbean people to contribute to these processes.

The network is a voluntary sector organisation that acts as the umbrella and coordinating body for the African and Caribbean communities in Glasgow. The Network's headquarters are in Osborne Street in the city centre: it is run by a board, all of whom have additional roles in supporting the African–Caribbean community. The Network also has a clear cultural remit and in September 2006 a festival celebrating African and Caribbean life and culture took place in the Albion Street centre.

Still working hard to uphold its remit, since 2014 the network launched, monthly, what it terms a 'talent incubation' show at their quarters. The aim of this was to unearth and promote genuine talent amongst the African and Caribbean community in the city and beyond.

At any time, there are more than 40 organisations affiliated to the Network, including, for example, Umoja, a self-help arts project that was set up in 2001. This community development group welcomed African women refugees and asylum seekers who had been housed in Glasgow on their own with children. The group met weekly and was involved in a range of practical and artistic events for several years.

Another body linked to the Network is the @frican Media Group (@MG). This was founded in 2005 as a new pan-African organisation of journalists, artists, musicians and other media-related professionals. It is designed to meet the informational needs of newly settled African communities. During 2005 and 2006 @MG ran community film screenings in collaboration with Glasgow Film Theatre, Glasgow Anti-Racist Alliance (GARA), Camcorder Guerillas and the Alliance Française de Glasgow.

The African and Caribbean Network was also pro-active in 2007 – the bicentenary of the abolition of the slave trade – organising a Freedom Walk festival amongst other things. Many cities across the United Kingdom arranged events to mark the anniversary of this shameful period in British history, including Glasgow, with the City Council sponsoring several initiatives around the city.

The African and Caribbean Network's aims were complemented by those of GARA. This organisation,which served the anti-racist movement, merged into the current body to become CRER – the Coalition for Equality and Rights.

In 2007 GARA also staged a series of special events to mark the abolition bicentenary. GARA received the Lifeline Expedition March as this major national effort reached Glasgow, the marchers wearing symbolic yokes and chains. This was the Sankofa Reconciliation Walk, so named from the African Akan culture, in which *sankofa* means 'we must learn from the past to build for the future'. The march, which concluded in

George Square, took in various locations in the city that had a past association with the slave trade, and now with the black history tours run by GARA. On the evening prior to the march, GARA hosted a Slavery Reparations debate in Glasgow City Chambers.

The declared purpose of the Glasgow Anti-Racist Alliance is to challenge racism and inequality in all aspects of life, particularly where these affect young people: 'If you don't challenge racism – who will'. The scope of the organisation is extensive, both in their own work and in partnership with many other groups. GARA sponsored the 7/84 Theatre Company in the making of a short film, *Challenge Racism*, which was shown in the Scottish Parliament, and also commissioned the Bird of Paradise Theatre Company to take a tour of the show *Whistleblower* to companies, colleges and voluntary organisations. In September 2006 GARA organised the Race and Regeneration Conference in St Andrews in the Square in Glasgow: its aim was to examine the degree to which race equality had permeated regeneration strategies. For some time it also produced *Black Perspectives*, a newsletter covering youth and race issues in Scotland. For example, GARA ran a politician shadowing scheme, designed to cultivate budding political talent in the young: the scheme provides participants with training in local Scottish and UK government, public speaking and anti-racism. The full extent of the work of this body was to be found on the GARA website (www.gara.org.uk).

Each year in Glasgow, GARA also supported the St Andrews Day March and Rally Against Racism and Fascism, and it continued to be the main organiser of Black History Month in the city. Museum and library venues across the city run a large programme of events. Glasgow Film Theatre, Glasgow University and several other arts and media groups were also engaged in hosting relevant events. As the Foreword to the programme stated:

> It is a unique opportunity to learn about, discuss and honour the role that black people have played in shaping Glasgow's history.

The programme is extensive and diverse, ranging from lectures, discussions, tours, poetry sessions, films and musical events in the Royal Concert Hall and other venues, and from subjects as diverse as the role of empire to footballing heroes. Overall, Black History Month is a valuable evocation of the role of black people throughout history, and, in particular, of their connections with Glasgow. In 2007 Black History Month had a particular resonance in the bicentenary year of the abolition.

In 2006, an informative event, amongst many, was the African Highlights Tour in the newly refurbished Kelvingrove Museum, which demonstrated much of contribution made to civilisation by African culture past and present, and in particular a recent acquisition, the Pot of Life. This is a modern bronze made in Benin City in recognition of the traditional art forms of the historic kingdom of Benin, now Southern Nigeria. The sculpture was commissioned in 2005 by Glasgow City Council and designed by Lucky Oboh, an artist living in the city. This sculpture, an example of the art of Nigeria, commissioned by the City Council, and created by an African artist in the city, highlights the inclusive and multi-cultural nature of Glasgow today.

In the Merchant City

I lounge at café table in cold
sun, sip bitter coffee, wipe froth from
lips with snowy cotton, savour
a cigarette.

Jamaica, Virginia, West Indies, Barbados

　　Faint at my back between colonnades
　　a cane tap taps,
　　gold headed. Voices mutter
　　of uncertainty
　　of tides. Sugar Princes mull
　　over the price of slaves,
　　the cost of cargo.
　　Capes swirl crimson above private
　　pavements. Chandlers, victualers,
　　scrabble in gutters.
　　Downstream, out of sight,
　　gulls keen, the river sucks greedily.

Spiers, Buchanan, Cunningham, Glassford.

In the Style City's crystal galleries
trade bleeds on.

FINOLA SCOTT

CHAPTER 2

The Glasgow Highlanders

THE GLASGOW HISTORIES tell us of 'a few Highland gentlemen' who had decided to settle in the city by the early 1700s. They were not very many, but the traffic was increasing and an inn, The Black Bull on Argyle Street, was opened specially to cater for the needs of the Highlanders when their coaches arrived in Glasgow. In 1727 the Glasgow Highland Society was founded and in 1767 a church was opened on Queen Street, in which the services were conducted in Gaelic.

The Glasgow Highland Society was established to raise funds for educating the sons of Highlanders in Glasgow and for putting them to apprenticeships. The boys were also supplied with clothes, including a 'dark blue bonnet', which they had to wear so that the members of the society would recognise them at all times and keep a check on their behaviour in public. The society continued its work for many years and by 1861 was educating and caring for 800 boys and girls. By now it was also giving weekly sums of money to Highland families at times of illness or unemployment, and as the number of Highland people in Glasgow rose and increasing demands were made upon the charity, it is not surprising that the society was in debt by 1861. The directors made an appeal both for more money and new members, to help support the large numbers of Highlanders who were still arriving in Glasgow looking for work:

> To the enlightened Citizens of Glasgow they beg leave with great respect to say that the Highland population constitutes a very large and valuable proportion of the working classes of the city and neighbourhood. They are to be found in all the public works and every department of labour. It becomes, therefore, a matter of vast importance to the best interests of the community that the children of this numerous body should be well trained and educated...
>
> The Directors look especially for countenance and support to Highland proprietors and gentlemen resident throughout the Highlands, from whose estates, and from the lands of whose fathers, very many poor people are at present removing to this city in quest of employment, and whose families possess the most tender and powerful claims on their compassion and charity.

Most of the people came from beyond what is known as the 'Highland Line' (see page 19), a part of Scotland that was difficult to reach and where the land was rough and hard to cultivate. The soil was poor and the climate could be severe and, for most people, earning a living from the land was a continual struggle for survival. By the mid 1700s it was becoming clear that the old agricultural methods and the traditional ways of dividing up the land from generation to generation would no longer continue to support an increasing population, and people began to leave the Highlands to search for work in the rapidly developing cities. More people were driven to leave, however, after the 1745 Jacobite uprising in the Highlands in support of Charles Edward Stewart (Bonnie Prince Charlie).

For over 200 years, Scotland had been largely Protestant in religion, with the exception of some of the Western Isles, and from 1603 the kings of Scotland were also kings of England. The Jacobite rebellion, which sought to put the Roman Catholic James Stewart (father of Charles) back on the throne, ended in defeat of the Highland forces at Culloden in 1746. After Culloden, the Westminster government determined to subdue the Highlanders once and for all, and Parliament passed the 'Rebellion Statutes'. These laws made it a crime for Highlanders to carry weapons, wear the tartan or play the bagpipes, and those caught breaking the law could be transported to the 'American Plantations'. Detachments of soldiers were posted throughout the Highlands to compel obedience, but people found ways to confuse their watchdogs:

REPORT from Capt.-Lieut. GEORGE SEMPILL, in Lord George Beauclerck's Regiment, dated Locharkaig, Oct. 13, 1755.

I have a report from the officer commanding in North and South Morer, that the inhabitants of those countries begin to wear instead of breeches, stuff trousers, much after the form of those that seamen use, but not longer than the kilt or philibeg.

I am at a loss whether to look upon that as part of the Highland dress, and take notice of such people as offenders against the law.

Nothing else extraordinary has happened in this district since the last report.

Many Lowlanders, and the English, saw the Highlanders as a lawless, barbaric people who needed to be tamed, by force if necessary. One soldier who was posted in the North, Major James Wolfe (later General Wolfe), hated the place and the people, and longed to be in North America instead, where his regiment was fighting off the French to keep the colony of Nova Scotia. He wrote to a fellow officer there:

> I imagine that two or three Highland companies might be of use. They are hardy, intrepid, accustomed to a rough country, *and no great mischief if they fall...* [my emphasis] a people better governed by fear.

Wolfe saw the Highlanders as nothing more than useful 'cannon fodder', and it would be no loss if they died capturing foreign territory, as they were such a wild and troublesome people at home. Many Highlanders did join the new Highland regiments that were set up at that time, but many were also 'pressed' – virtually kidnapped – into the King's service in the various parts of the world where British power was being exercised. Many Highlanders also emigrated to Nova Scotia and other colonies, but large numbers made their way to the cities, and to Glasgow in particular.

Glasgow had rejoiced at the Jacobite defeat at Culloden; the city was doing well out of the trade resulting from the Union and was not interested in the Stewart cause, but by the end of the century things were less promising. The city's population was rising very rapidly and a disastrous harvest in 1782, bringing the threat of famine to country districts, only added to the flow of immigrants into the city. Glasgow was described as 'a magnet attracting immigrants from distressed rural areas'.

One group of Highlanders who settled in the city, at least for a time, was bound originally for America. When their ship was wrecked, the passengers landed, destitute, in Glasgow. Most were Gaelic-speaking Catholics from Glengarry in Inverness-shire, and through the good work of their priest, Father MacDonnell, employment was found for about 600 of the new arrivals. When Britain's war with France interrupted the export trade and threw these people out of work, Father MacDonnell went to the government and gained a promise of land in Canada for those of his people who could get there to claim it. The priest went with them and the Canadian settlement of Glengarry was founded. The Glasgow Highland Society did not, in general, approve of emigration as a solution to the Highlanders' problems, since usually it was only the most active and healthy people with their children who were allowed to go, leaving the weak and elderly behind to fend for themselves, often tearing families apart.

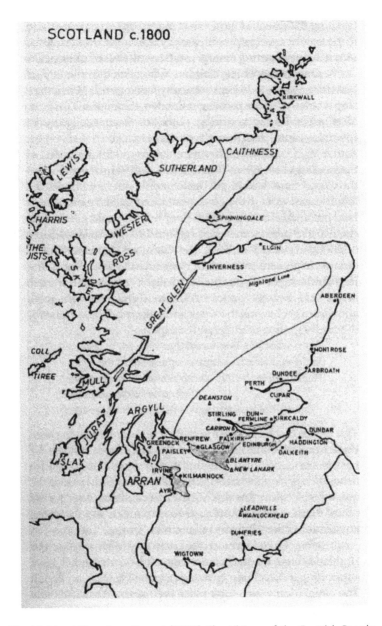

The Highland Line, from Smout (1969) *The History of the Scottish People.*

Even so, it has been said that:

In the eighteenth century people go from the Highlands, in the nineteenth century they are sent.

Scottish Geographical, May 1934

This means that however urgent their reasons for leaving their homes or their country, people in the 18th century did have some choice, little though it may have been. But for thousands of people in the Highlands in the early part of the 19th century this was not the case, and they were forced out of their homes and off their land to make way for sheep and cattle, as the 'Highland Clearances' began.

After Culloden and the new repressive laws, the Highlands were relatively more peaceful, but the problems of supporting a constantly growing population were no easier. The emigration that took place then seemed to make little difference. At this time, moreover, the war with France led to large increases in the value of home-produced goods, and wool was becoming a very profitable product. Highland landowners saw opportunities to make great sums of money from their estates by turning them over to sheep farms. This meant, however, that the people who had lived and worked on these lands for generations had to be removed. Some landowners did what they could to make the process of eviction less distressing for their tenants, but in other cases the eviction of people from their homes was carried out with the utmost callousness and brutality. The most notorious example of this was on the estates of Sutherland, where the scars left on the memory of the people remain to this day.

Between 1807 and 1829 agents acting on behalf of the Countess of Sutherland expelled up to 10,000 people from their homes to make way for sheep. Historians have suggested that while the Sutherlands did spend money on projects that might have provided other income for some of their tenants, the fact that they lived in England and only visited their Sutherland estates once every four or five years allowed their agents a free hand in the manner in which the Clearances were conducted. A later inquiry said of such 'absentee landowners' that:

By deserting their houses and properties and resorting to the gayer and more fashionable societies of the South they acquire habits of expense more to the kindness of their hearts than to the extent of their income.

Remarks on Evils Affecting Highlands & Islands, 1838

The new breed of Highland landowners needed a great deal of money to live in the style of English aristocrats, and if sheep farming could provide it they were often willing to turn a blind eye to the miseries caused to the people whom the sheep were replacing. Much of what happened on the Sutherland lands was exposed by one of their tenants, Donald McLeod, a stonemason and a literate and outspoken man. He wrote that:

> Down from feudal times the inhabitants of the hills and straths of Sutherlandshire... looked upon the farms they occupied as their own, from their ancestors.

Now they were being cruelly evicted, their homes pulled down and burned, and the tenants sent elsewhere to rebuild their houses with their own hands.

The most infamous Sutherland agent was Patrick Sellar, who evicted people with such ruthlessness that he even had houses set on fire while the people were still inside. In 1816 Sellar was brought to trial for murder and fire-raising but was acquitted because, as McLeod said, 'those interested in suppressing inquiry are numerous, powerful and unsparing in the use of influence'. Sellar's trial was not fairly conducted as there were few witnesses, those of which were Gaelic-speaking while the trial was conducted in English. The beginning of the trial documents show a little of what Sellar was accused.

> Patrick Sellar, now or lately residing in Culmaily, in the parish of Golspie, and shire of Sutherland, and under factor for the Most Noble the Marquis and Marchioness of Stafford. You are indicted and accused, at the instance of Archibald Colquoun of Killermont, his Majesty's Advocate for his Majesty's interest: THAT ALBEIT, by the laws of this and every other well-governed realm, CULPABLE HOMICIDE, as also OPPRESSION and REAL INJURY, more particularly the wickedly and maliciously setting on fire and burning, or causing and procuring to be set on fire and burnt, a great extent of heath and pasture, on which a number of small tenants and other poor persons maintain their cattle, to the great injury and distress of the said persons; the violently turning, or causing and procuring to be turned out of their habitations, a number of the said tenants and other poor people, especially aged, infirm, and impotent persons, and pregnant women, and cruelly depriving them of all cover or shelter, to their great distress, and imminent

danger of their lives; the wickedly and maliciously setting on fire, burning, pulling down, and demolishing, or causing and procuring to be set on fire, burnt, pulled down, and demolishing, the dwelling houses, barns, kilns, sheds and other buildings, lawfully occupied by the said persons whereby they themselves are turned out without cover or shelter, as aforesaid, and the greater part of their animals and crops is destroyed, from the want of the cover and necessary accommodation for securing and managing the same; and the wantonly setting on fire, burning, otherwise destroying or causing and procuring to be set on fire, burnt, and otherwise destroyed, growing corn, shelter, furniture, money and other effects, the property, and goods in the lawful possession of the said tenants and other poor persons; all are crimes of a heinous nature and severely prosecuted.

The indictment goes on to specify the exact days of the months of March, April and May in 1814 on which Patrick Sellar had carried out these actions against particular tenants and employees and names the lands on which they had lived.

The majority of tenants treated in this way were 'tenants at will', that is, they could be thrown out 'at will' of the person who owned the land. Eventually, almost the whole population of Sutherland was driven to build new villages by the coast, where they were crowded on to small plots of land and expected to catch fish to earn a living and pay their rent, a skill of which very few of them had experience. Donald McLeod maintained that by 1827 the depopulation of the Highlands was achieved, and the land had passed into the hands of a few rich and powerful men. The strong feelings of those so badly treated can be seen in these lines, written over 100 years ago:

Can Law be Law when based on Wrong?
Can Law be Law when for the strong?
Can Law be Law when landlords stand
Rack-renting mankind off the land?
By 'Law' a landlord can become
The ghost of every Crofter's home;
By 'Law' their little cots can be
Dark dens of dirt and misery;
By 'Law' the tax upon their toil

Is squandered on an alien soil;
By 'Law' their daughters, sons and wives,
Are doomed to slavish drudgery's lives;
By 'Law' Eviction's dreadful crimes
Are possible in Christian times;
By 'Law' a spendthrift lord's intents
Are met by drawing higher rents;
By 'Law' all food-producing glens
Are changed from farms to cattle pens:
This is your 'Law' whereby a few
Are shielded in the deeds they do.

St Michael and the Preacher, Rev. Donald MacSiller

During this time, many people preferred to emigrate, or to try for a better life by moving south, and Donald McLeod was no exception. He paid for his outspokenness by being accused of owing money and was evicted from his home – his furniture thrown out, his doors and windows boarded up and his family left without shelter. After this, McLeod moved to Edinburgh and later emigrated to Canada.

Many evicted tenants, however, made their way to Glasgow, to swell the ranks of the poor in the city, which was becoming overcrowded and insanitary. In 1836–7 famine struck once again in the North, and the condition of the Highlanders, both at home and in the cities, caused such grave concern that an official inquiry was set up. The *Report of the Glasgow Committee for the Relief of Destitute Inhabitants of the Highlands* described conditions in the Highlands and it is apparent that, bad as the city was, it was probably no worse than that which the Highlander was leaving behind. By now, the poorer people's diet was 80 per cent potatoes, and their homes described as:

...wretched and miserable, little more than a hut... one end occupied by the family and the other by the cow if they have one... or the pig... all using one door. The fire peat or turf, is in the centre of the floor and the smoke escapes through a hole in the roof: the floor is simply the soil... hardly any clothes... bedclothes turned into garments to wear...

The *Report* also stressed that in the whole area of the Highlands there was neither hospital nor poorhouse, little education and practically no industry. A table from the *Report* (see page 26) gives only a sample of the number of people in Highland parishes who were willing to choose the risk of emigration in order to escape their poverty.

For those destitute people who chose to come to Glasgow, however, much of the attraction of the city was its industry; but Highlanders were unused to the ways of factory or mill, and besides, according to the *Report*, the Highlander was already sorely handicapped by his Gaelic language:

> We cannot conceive of a more helpless being than a Highlander, who knows only his native language, endeavouring to push his way among the people of England or the low counties of Scotland.

In spite of this assessment, it was not impossible for the Highlander to 'push his way' into work in Glasgow, for by this time the city had a massive cotton industry. In the American War of Independence of 1775–83, the tobacco-producing colonies had thrown off English rule and the trade more or less came to an end, but canny Glasgow merchants, who had made their money from slaves or tobacco, now saw the possibilities of investing in cotton manufacture. The damp, temperate climate of the Glasgow area provided ideal conditions, the development of James Watt's steam engine provided a source of power, and the constant stream of immigrants from the Highlands and Ireland provided the huge labour force that was required for the mass production of cotton.

A highland dwelling, known as a black house.

By 1831 it is believed that there were about 39,000 Highlanders in Glasgow, but it was not necessarily an easy life that they came to in the wake of the Clearances, recurring famines, or the failure of the potato crop in 1845. Wealthier Glaswegians were moving out of the centre into the cleaner air and wider spaces of the suburbs: dirty, overcrowded tenements – some hastily erected to house the vast labour force needed by the industry – were now occupied by the immigrants, who were exposed to the various epidemic diseases that struck the city with dreadful regularity (see page 26).

Between 1818 and 1852 Glasgow experienced five outbreaks of typhus fever besides the more common diseases of tuberculosis, diphtheria and smallpox. In 1832 and 1848–9, moreover, the population was decimated by outbreaks of cholera. Disease is no respecter of persons but the newly arrived Highlander would have had little immunity to diseases that owed their spread and effects to slum housing conditions and inadequate water supplies. The *Annual Mortality Report* for Glasgow, dealing with January 1849, stated:

> that during the month of January there were no fewer than 3,100 burials within the various Cemeteries of Glasgow, of which there were 1,780 from Cholera and 1,320 from other diseases, and when we compare these with the burials of January 1848, which amounted to 1,674, we find, in spite of the existence of the then prevailing typhus or famine fever, that the burials in January 1849, were 1,426 more than in January 1848. It is, perhaps, almost unnecessary to add, that no previous month in the whole history of Glasgow ever exhibited so high a figure of mortality as January 1849; for, assuming the same rate to have continued throughout the whole year, it would have shewn an annual mortality for Glasgow of about 36,000, and which to estimated population would have been as one out of every seven!

Highlanders worked in the cotton mills and many of the women and girls were employed in the bleaching and dyeing works of the textile industry. Many Highland men, however, preferred to join the Glasgow Police Force rather than be shut up in factory or mill for 12 or 14 hours a day.

The police force was first established in Glasgow in 1800 and the Highland policeman was to become a familiar figure on the streets of

128 [TABLE IX.

Name of Parish.	Disposition to Emigrate.
1 Barvas ⎫	At least ⅓ of the people if means provided
2 Lochs ⎪	Yes—young men and women disposed to emig.
3 Stornoway ⎬ LEWIS	Cottars and labourers are disposed
4 Uig ⎭	Not disposed
5 Barra - - -	
6 Harris - -	Some of the destitute if clothes are furnished
7 Bracadale ⎤	1000 anxious
8 Durinish ⎪	Very great to America
9 Kilmuir ⎪	Yes—in whole families
10 Sleat ⎬ SKYE	Yes—to Canada
11 Snizort ⎪	Great disposition
12 Stencholl ⎦	Young men if means provided
13 North Uist - -	Great if means provided
14 South Uist - -	
⎡ Canna - - -	
⎪ Eigg - - -	The whole to America if means
15 ⎬ Muck - - -	provided
⎣ Rum - - -	
16 Coll - - -	100 poor and working classes
17 Lismore - -	
18 Appin - - ⎫	Not much disposed
19 Kilmore and Kilbride ⎬	
20 Torosay - -	Most of small tenants and cottars and families
21 Ulva - -	Yes—to America with free passage ¼
22 Tyree - -	1000 would if means provided
23 Iona - -	Very few
24 Applecross - -	Yes—in whole families if means provided
25 Gairloch - -	600 single men and crofters families
26 Glenshiel - -	40 families to Canada if ⅔ of expense advanced
27 Carnack - -	12 families if means given
28 Kincardine - -	Very little
29 Kintail - -	Young people in great numbers
30 Lochalsh - -	No anxiety
31 Lochbroom without Ullapool	Very much of all descriptions
32 Lochcarron - -	Disposed to emigration
33 Poolewe - -	Very little disposition
34 Shieldag - -	200 families if means provided
35 Ullapool - -	1500 to America if means provided
36 Urquhart and Glenmoriston	Disposed to emigrate to Australia
37 Ballachulish -	30 or 40 crofter's families
38 Boleskin and Abertarf	20 families
39 Croich - -	
40 Daviot - - -	
41 Glenelg - -	One fifth if means provided
42 Kilmorack - -	Many if provided with means
43 Kingussie without Insh	Many if means provided
44 Kirkhill - -	....
45 Kirtarlity - -	....
46 Laggan - -	Yes—if means provided
47 Moy and Dalarossie -	A few anxious
48 Rothiemurchus -	135 labourers and tenants
49 Ardnamurchan witht. Sunart	Some are disposed to emigrate
50 Arasaig - -	Disposition—labourers and shepherds would
51 Craignish - -	No disposition to emigrate
52 Morvern - -	If proper scheme proposed

One of the tables from *The Report of the Glasgow Committee for the Relief of Destitute Inhabitants of the Highlands.*

Glasgow for very many years to come. William Sinclair, a farm servant from Caithness who joined the police in 1852, is just one example of those who are to be found in the records of Glasgow Police. He rose to sergeant and was rewarded with 7/6d (37p) in 1858 for 'apprehending a child shipper and returned convict'. William spent almost 40 years as a Glasgow policeman.

Perhaps it was their different language, making the English they spoke a second language, perhaps it was their tendency to stick together and their unfamiliarity with city ways, but the Highlander became, for a time at least, an object of criticism in Lowland cities. *The Scotsman* newspaper was expressing a common, if unfounded, belief in 1846, when it declared:

> It is the fact that morally and intellectually the Highlanders are
> an inferior race to the Lowland Saxons.

Historians suggest that Lowland Scots who envied the more powerful English, yet could not afford to criticise them, vented much of their prejudices on the Highland (and the growing number of Irish) immigrants in the cities, many of whose problems had been brought about by forces beyond their control. These prejudices were revealed in cruel jokes that created an image of the Highlander as stupid and slow, his accent comical and his Gaelic language gibberish.

The Poet's Box was one of many shops selling penny song sheets, some of which made fun of the plight of the Highlander arriving in the city for the first time. One example, from 1874, began:

> O, her nainsel cam frae ta Isle o' Skye,
> Whar she was herd ta sheep and kye,
> But she cam tae Glasco toon till try
> An' be a Hieland Polisman.
> When she'll arrive at the Broomielaw,
> She'll dinna ken whar till gang ava,
> For she was dumbfounded at what she'll saw
> When she cam to be a Polisman.

The Bailie, a weekly magazine published in Glasgow for many years, was confident in the knowledge that it was safe to amuse its readers by making fun of the Highlander. Auchtray McTavish x71, the Hielan' Polisman, featured regularly in the magazine.

In the ground, or land, at the back of tenements (the Backlands), small, inadequately built houses which quickly became slums, were erected to serve the growing population of Glasgow.

Photograph by Thomas Annan.

I woot wantit my prose sooner for a week than miss ta sports of ta forse on Saturday whateffer; for pesides ta telight of ta dancing, wheelbarrows, cotch ta sief, opstacles, sack race, tossing ta caber, ant eferysing forpye, ter wass ta pleesure of tooking ta road hame wis a Lipton's ham pelow her two oxter, ant a gelly dish or a cake pasket in her sporran too forpye.

The Bailie

Polisman.

A great deal of real Gaelic, however, would be spoken when the Highlanders congregated at their favourite meeting place in the city, by the Clyde at the bottom of Jamaica Street. On Sundays or other 'off duty' times, Highlanders knew there was a good chance that they would meet someone from their own island or village there and they would contact friends and exchange news. By 1935, however, the Highlanders' meeting place had changed, and they would gather under Central Station bridge in Argyle Street, known by Glaswegians for many years as the 'Hielanman's Umbrella'.

Well into the 20th century, in fact, Highlanders were still moving into Glasgow in considerable numbers. Yet another famine in the winter of 1923–4 brought many West Highlanders into the already overcrowded city and into conditions that they must have found both alarming and depressing.

In 1917 a Royal Commission investigating housing conditions described Glasgow as 'a clotted mass of slums', and by this time the city had also earned the unenviable title of 'Cancer of Empire'. These descriptions were far removed from the pleasing account of the city given by Daniel Defoe, when he had visited 200 years earlier. Much of the problem came from the fact that a period of dramatic growth had taken place, unaccompanied by the careful planning and organisation necessary to avoid the social problems that came with rapid industrial expansion, and it was easier to blame the large numbers of immigrants who had entered Glasgow rather than examine the deeper causes of poverty and slum housing.

Besides accounting for a large part of the police force, Highlanders worked in all the heavy industries and made their contribution to the products of these industries that made Glasgow famous throughout the world – ships, locomotives, industrial steam boilers and many other heavy engineering constructions. Many Highland girls also came to the city to join the nursing profession or enter domestic service, and young people also came to continue their education in the colleges or the university. Men, particularly from the islands, built up a strong tradition of seamanship and filled all ranks of the Merchant Service, with Glasgow their home port.

When Highlanders met and spoke their own language it obviously sounded unusual to the ear of the Glasgow listener, but it was not respected as simply a language that was different, it was laughed at and The Bailie would make mock of the Gaelic language as meaningless sounds as in 'MacOolachan and ta Pone' 1890. *The Bailie.*

In time, various organisations and associations were formed for the Highland population in Glasgow, among them the Highlanders' Institute, which opened in Elmbank Street in 1925. The Institute provided a hostel and library and was a place where people could meet their friends – the building now houses the Volunteer Centre. The Institute later moved to Berkeley Street, but has closed in recent years. There are other organisations in the city that keep Gaelic culture alive, however, such as the 'territorial' associations that provide a social function for people from particular places – Lewis and Harris, and Mull and Iona, for example. These associations run dances and ceilidhs, maintaining the contact between those who have been born in the Highlands and Islands and those born in Glasgow of Highland descent. There are also a number of organisations devoted to the preservation and encouragement of the Gaelic language: besides the Glasgow Gaelic Musical Association there are several choirs, including the Hebridean Gaelic Choir, the Glasgow Islay Choir and the Govan Gaelic Choir. In the city a Gaelic Drama Festival and a Glasgow Local Mod are held annually.

In several city churches the service is preached in the Gaelic language and over the years there have been a number of interesting developments in support of the language and culture of the Gaels. Outwith the formal school system, the mother tongue is fostered at the earliest stages in play-groups for under-5s and the language is taught as a subject and employed as a medium at both primary and secondary stages in some Glasgow schools.

The 2001 Census figure for those in Glasgow who speak, read or understand Gaelic was more than 10,000, a considerable increase from the 1991 figure of 6,500. Some of these will be among the much smaller number of Highlanders who still move in to make the city their home, but by far the greatest number are the 'Glasgow Highlanders', the children or descendants of those Highlanders who have settled in Glasgow over the last 200 years, and a very small part of whose story has been told here. Much of this increase must be accounted for by the fact that there has been a radical reappraisal of Gaelic's role in Scotland for the 21st century. However the most recent figure, in the 2011 Census, accounting for those who can speak, read and write Gaelic, stood at 3,476. This figure is for the city but the census returns for Scotland as a whole show 32,000 plus who could speak, read and write Gaelic, with a significant number competent in one or two elements of the language, such as speaking and understanding without reading. In total, the number of people in Scotland who had some degree of skill in the language actually numbered 187,156.

The passing of the Gaelic Language (Scotland) Act, which came into force in 2006, was a major milestone in the history of Gaelic's place in the community. The Act is thorough and far-reaching, and provided for the setting up of a corporate body, the *Bòrd na Gàidhlig*:

> The Act establishes a body... to promote the use and understanding of the Gaelic language and enables the *Bòrd* to require certain public bodies to prepare and implement plans which will set out how they will use the Gaelic language in the exercise of their functions.

Further to this, amongst other duties, the board is required to monitor and report to the Scottish Ministers on the implementation of the European Charter for Regional or Minority Languages (1992).

The board also has a seminal role in securing the status of the Gaelic language as an official language of Scotland: 'commanding equal respect to the English language through increasing the number of speakers.' As part of this remit, the board was also required to submit a National Gaelic Language Plan to the Executive within an agreed timescale.

It is, moreover, empowered to issue guidance on the provision and development of Gaelic education, and an important innovation was the opening of the new *Sgoil Ghàidhlig Ghlaschu* in August 2006, the first ever stand alone Gaelic-medium secondary school. The school is based in Woodside Campus, on the site of the former Woodside Secondary in Berkeley Street, close to the city centre. The school's aim is to deliver all curricular areas through the medium of Gaelic, in pre-5, primary and secondary education. In effect, teaching and learning in Gaelic from the age of three to the age of 18. In August, 52 children entered Primary 1 at the school, 60 per cent of whose parents are not Gaelic speakers. Pre-5 Gaelic medium provision is still offered at several other nursery schools in the city.

In addition to the language, the education department promotes a full programme of cultural opportunities for children attending Gaelic-medium provision, including tuition in piping and traditional song and dance, and pupils are also given the opportunity to participate in the Mod, local festivals and the annual Celtic Connections festival in Glasgow. There is an Adviser in Gaelic Education in the city council, and there is an indication that the language is being opened up to a whole new range of learners as parents are influenced by their children's experience in the medium.

In 2005 and 2006, during *Comunn na Gàidhlig's* Gaelic Schools Week, a series of visits were arranged for pupils to the Scottish Parliament at Holyrood. In October 2006, George Reid, the then Presiding Officer, welcomed the announcement by the *Bòrd na Gàidhlig* that the Parliament is one of six public bodies required to develop a formal Gaelic Language Plan under the Act. Proceedings are published in Gaelic on the parliamentary website, and all printed educational publications for schools are available in Gaelic, together with the majority of public information leaflets and Parliament's *Annual Report*.

And in Glasgow, at the publishing of the Gaelic Arts Strategy for 2006–2009, Boyd Robertson, Reader in Gaelic Education at Strathclyde University and Chairman of *An Lòchran*, commented:

> Glasgow and Gaelic are inextricably linked. The city has been home to a large community of Gaelic speakers since the 18th century and it has a special place in the hearts and minds of Gaels everywhere.

He goes on to point out that one in every six Gaelic speakers in Scotland reside in or around Glasgow.

An Lòchran ('The Lantern') aims to take Gaelic arts in the city to a new level and to bring Gaelic culture within reach of the wider population: supporting this is the role of the Gaelic Arts Development Officer based within Glasgow City Council. The strategy also stresses that a vital component is the establishment of a cultural centre, which would provide a hub for Gaelic artistic activity and a creative space for the community.

The organisation was formed in 1999 and through various developments reached the point of setting out its strategy for the years 2006–9 through a series of 'core, strategic and project' activities in that time. Within the strategy, *An Lòchran* advocates an approach that ensures traditional art forms continue to thrive and reach out to new audiences, but also, through a new agenda

> of research, historical and cultural exploration… will enable greater understanding of Gaelic identity… and a secure and sustainable Gaelic arts infrastructure.

Comunn na Gaidhlig.

Lios mor.

A flagship event under the auspices of *An Lòchran* was the 'Flower of the West', a comprehensive event consisting of a touring exhibition, talks, a concert and children's art workshops in Glasgow and the Western Isles, in May 2005.

An Lòchran's Gaelic arts programme is set out in the online newsletter, including community events such as *Fèis Glaschu* (a festival of music held during the Easter and October school breaks) and *Ceòl's Craic* (a monthly Gaelic club with performances from professional artists), both of which are held in the Centre for Contemporary Arts on Sauchiehall Street, and Glasgow's annual West End Festival in June, with workshops in language, fiddle, accordion, *bodhran* and Gaelic song.

In 2007 *An Lochran* commissioned an Economic Impact Study of Gaelic Arts to the City of Glasgow. The research was conducted by Glasgow Caledonian University, with support from Glasgow City Council. With many of the more venerable Gaelic institutions in Glasgow still in good heart – the musical pubs such as the *Lios Mhor* in Partick, the formal choirs, the Highland Associations – together with the continuance of Gaelic religious services, the outlook for the language and culture of the Gael in the city is perhaps at its most optimistic. And, undeniably, a great accolade for all the efforts that have gone to bring about this state of affairs must have been the designation by the Scottish Government of 2007 as The Year of Highland Culture.

Developments since that time included the launching of the Scottish Gaelic television channel – Alba – broadcasting nationally seven hours daily. And in April 2016, a renewed contribution to the language and culture was pronounced in a second Gaelic Language Plan, by VisitScotland, the nation's official tourism body. Pledging a three year period in which it sets out to fulfil its duty to help deliver the objectives of all other relevant parties to the fostering of the language and culture, Riddell Graham, a director of VisitScotland, said his organisation was 'keen to support the promotion and recognition, of Gaelic, not only as an important part of the country's heritage, but as a living language.'

It is all a very far cry from the derogatory cartoons of MacOolachan.

CHAPTER 3

The Irish in Glasgow

IN THE 1840S AND 1850S, Irish people were flocking into Glasgow at the rate of several thousand a week, and to some people it seemed that the city would not be able to survive this 'invasion'. But the Irish had been coming to Scotland long before this: in 1689 the Committee of Glasgow Churches spoke of 'a great number of poor people lately come from Ireland to Glasgow', and the ministers who wrote the *Statistical Account of Scotland* at the end of the 18th century expressed their concern about a flood of poor Irish with 'a superstitious religion and alien customs' into the textile parishes of the West of Scotland.

It had long been customary for Irish people to come to Scotland to work at the harvest. They would come for the season and return with their earnings to Ireland. This traffic increased when the new steamboats provided a cheap passage across the Irish Sea. The first cross-channel steamboat in the world sailed from Glasgow to Belfast in 1818. By 1833 fares were so cheap that even the poorest could find passage to Glasgow.

That fine new steamer *The Antelope* is now carrying passengers from Belfast to Glasgow at the reduced fares of 1/ for the cabin and 6d for the steerage. On her arrival at Greenock on Saturday morning she had upwards of a thousand of the most wretched of misgoverned Ireland's poor upon her decks.

Glasgow Argus, 1833

The obvious question is why was it necessary for the Irish to come to Scotland to find work? A clue to the answer is seen in the *Glasgow Argus* report, which suggested that Ireland was 'misgoverned'. Much of Ireland was desperately poor and conditions for the majority of the population were very bad. At a time when Britain, and much of Scotland in particular, was making great advances in agriculture and industry, Ireland was being left behind and was used instead to provide vast resources of cheap labour for British industry. As Irish people fled the poverty of their homeland to sell their labour elsewhere in Britain and abroad, they were responding to a situation that had been in the making for centuries.

As early as the 12th century, Ireland had experienced 'foreign' rule when much of the country was conquered by the English king. At this time, there was at least no religious conflict, because to be Christian in any part of Western Europe then was to be Roman Catholic. By the early 1600s, however, Protestant rule was introduced to the North of Ireland when Protestants from Scotland and England were settled in Ulster. Irish historians say that two Irelands were created when Ulster was settled; one Catholic and Gaelic speaking, the other Protestant and English speaking. By 1653, moreover, the Protestant forces of Oliver Cromwell had totally subjugated all of Ireland, and those Irish landowners who still rebelled against English rule had their land taken away from them. The importance of Ireland to England lay, to a large extent, in the fact that a Catholic Ireland was a temptation to England's Catholic enemies, such as Spain, and so it was therefore necessary for England to control Ireland. New Protestant landowners were thus given control of most of the land even though the people were Catholic, and the Irish Parliament was controlled by English or Anglo-Irish ministers. When the Irish people rebelled against British rule in 1798, the uprising was put down with much bloodshed. The Irish Parliament was abolished and in 1801 Ireland entered an Act of Union with Great Britain.

The Irish people were repressed politically, educationally and economically. Laws kept Irish Catholics out of parliament and they were not allowed to vote, hold public office or attend university. The British parliament, moreover, controlled the development of Irish industry and so there was little of it, with people mainly in rural occupations. As a conquered territory, Ireland was treated like a colony, and was excluded from the advantages of the Union, which might have brought some compensations. Unlike Scotland, Ireland was not allowed to trade with the overseas colonies, and we have already seen how much wealth this opportunity could bring. Instead, Ireland exported her labour as her people emigrated to wealthier lands.

During Britain's wars with France, vast increases in the price of corn encouraged Irish landowners to sub-let much of their land for growing corn. For these holdings they could charge high rents.

With a growing population there was much competition for these lands until rents reached the point where the poorer people were driven out because they simply could not afford such high rents. This situation was made much worse when Ireland, too, had Clearances similar to those carried out in the Scottish Highlands, and farms were turned over to dairy farming or cattle breeding, their produce going to feed the rapidly growing population of industrial Britain. When the Clearances began, the landlords, greedy for profit, often neglected the land and preferred, as one Irish historian, James Handley, puts it,

> ... shooting and hunting and swilling, keeping open house for their cronies and living far beyond their income.
>
> *The Irish in Scotland*, 1943

The owners often rented out bare, unimproved land; the tenant would reclaim the land from the bog, drain it and ditch it, and the landlord was then free to put up the rents because of the improvements, or evict those who could not afford the higher rents. Many landlords were, of course, absentees, with their lands in the control of agents. Conditions gradually declined until the great majority of the Irish population were living on small pieces of land, often little more than a garden, 'in miserable cabins, without windows and without chimneys' and living off their 'lumpers', the coarse potatoes that kept body and soul together for most of the year.

For thousands of people, therefore, it must have been a relief to escape once a year from such conditions to work at the harvest in Scotland or England. Not that the Irish were always welcome in Scotland – the Highlanders, for example, often resented their presence and saw them as competition for agricultural jobs. They were also resented because they would often work for very low wages, which were nevertheless an improvement on what they would have earned at home in Ireland. And occasionally, if an Irish harvester had bad times, or behaved foolishly with his wages, he would turn up at the Broomielaw in Glasgow begging his passage money home. In a shop known as the Poet's Box, there were many comic songs telling the story of innocent Irishmen being taken in by wily Glaswegians. The sorry tale of Barney Liggett is one such poem:

> It's from the harvest I took my way,
> After four weeks of hard shearing,
> I overtook hundreds that day.
> For Glasgow city they were steering,
> 'Twas in the Briggate I did see

Some lassies that were up to dodging,
Before I did begin my spree,
Near the Old Wynd I took up my lodging.
Ye shearers all if you be wise,
You'll take warning by Barney Liggett;
You'll find you're far off Paradise,
If you take lodgings in the Briggate.

The song goes on to tell how Barney had intended to take all his earnings home to Ireland, to 'Judy and the bairn', but his good intentions come to nothing when he falls into the clutches of some Glasgow girls who steal his money. For most, though, the seasonal work sent them home a little better off, as the *Glasgow Examiner* reported in 1845:

Immense numbers of Irish reapers have passed through Glasgow on their return from different parts of Scotland... on questioning a small party that looked exceedingly pleased we learned that each had saved about £3 of money which they were carrying home with ineffable delight... give Pat a good sickle and 12/- a week and he will disregard all weathers and finish his task and return home with his wages.

These Irish workers were, of course, coming to Scotland to meet a labour demand created by Scotland's expanding economy, and many would come to live here permanently when the harvesters went back to Ireland and spoke of the opportunities to be found in the developing industries in the towns. We have already seen, however, that no poor person coming to Glasgow, as it was then, would find excellent conditions or a pleasant quality of life, but the Irish immigrant was making a choice between bad conditions in Glasgow and even worse conditions at home in Ireland. Even so, Glasgow was becoming overcrowded and sordid; living conditions were on the way to becoming the worst in Britain and the Irish were pouring into the city in their thousands and making the problems worse. By 1831, it was estimated that there were over 35,000 Irish-born people in Glasgow.

By this time, the question of Irish immigration into Britain as a whole was worrying the churches, the charity organisations and indeed the government itself, and a Commission of Inquiry into the State of the Irish Poor in Great Britain was set up in 1835.

In Glasgow, the evidence of surgeons John Stirling and Moses Steven

Buchanan shows that the Irish were regarded as a people of very low class, in fact barely civilised. What is more, the Irish immigrants were also being blamed for many of the evils that were now afflicting Glasgow.

The dwellings of the Irish are poorer than those of the Scotch in the same class of life; more of them are huddled together; the houses are ill-furnished, ill-aired, and dirty in the extreme. The poor Irish frequently lie on the floor, on straw or shavings; frequently, however, they have beds. It is the practice for as many to sleep in the same bed as can be crowded into it – it is not uncommon for three or four to lie in the same bed – frequently three or four beds are in the same apartment, in which males and females sleep next to one another... The Irish are, in general, dirtier and less well clothed than the native population.

In consequence of the crowded state of the Irish lodging houses, typhus has prevailed in Glasgow among the Irish more extensively than among the Scotch. During the operations of the fever committees, they have often been obliged to shut up these lodging houses, and fumigate and whitewash them in order to prevent contagion, especially in spots where the Irish first come, from the steam-boats... generally speaking the dwellings of the Irish are a grade inferior in relation to furniture; the lowest part of the working population being Irish, we find that in comfort, education, and moral feeling, they are inferior to the Scotch; the Irish are more indifferent to education than the Scotch, and education does not prevail so extensively among them.

The Irish Poor in Great Britain

It was becoming obvious that Glasgow's social problems were getting out of hand, and in such a situation it was convenient to have a scapegoat. For many people, the Irish fitted the bill perfectly. Handley said the Irish:

were hardly treated like a race but rather like a rash; like a disease that had broken out upon the soil and must be suppressed... like measles.

The Irish in Scotland, 1943

In fact, it was considered desirable that the Irish be 'suppressed' for a number of reasons, not least because most of the immigrants were Roman Catholics. James Cleland, a prominent Glasgow citizen, wrote in 1837:

The increase in Roman Catholics has been very rapid. A Bill having been brought into Parliament in 1780 for repealing certain Penal Statutes against Roman Catholics alarm was so great that 85 Societies were formed to oppose the Bill. On... the day appointed for a National Fast a mob collected in Tureen Street and destroyed Mr Bagnell's pottery factory for no other reason than that he was a Catholic.

In 1785 when Bishop Hay came from Edinburgh to celebrate Mass with Catholics who had emigrated chiefly from the North Highlands they met in clandestine manner in the back room of a house... at the foot of Saltmarket.

Cleland: Tracts, 1837

Gradually, however, as the Catholic population of the city increased, Highland and Irish Roman Catholic churches were built; the first proper one on the Gallowgate in 1797, and by 1815 St Andrew's Cathedral on Clyde Street. But anti-Catholic disturbances in Glasgow were to be a feature for decades to come, mostly directed against the Irish. Much of the hostility was, of course, mixed with the idea that the Irish took away the jobs of the native population and kept wages down. Handley, the historian of the Irish in Scotland, argues that this ignored the fact that the Irish were often doing dirty, heavy jobs that the locals did not want anyway, working as colliers or labourers on railways and canals in conditions that were little above slavery.

By 1837, Cleland's report nevertheless shows that in Glasgow one out of every five paupers was Irish, and that the number was increasing. This situation was causing grave concern in the city. This in turn led to more investigations being conducted and reports written, which, if they did not solve the problem of the Irish poor, certainly recorded it for posterity. In 1841 an investigation was carried out by Captain Miller, the city's Superintendent of Police. In minute detail he recorded the situation of 1,038 destitute persons.

One of the tables from this investigation shows that in seven adjacent closes in High Street alone there were 65 households, with 14 at No. 80 and 26 at No. 100. It appears that there were 65 adults and 114 children in these seven closes, 68 of the children under 10 years old, but a closer look at the table shows that wives were not listed. Among the men, 13 had children, some as many as six, so we could assume another 13 women in these seven closes. A total of 192 people lived here, all in one-room dwellings, most of them smaller than 14 square feet (4.26 square metres).

Most of the households (36) were Scottish, and 28 were Glaswegian. Only seven households had arrived in the past ten years. Two-thirds of the households (43) were headed by widows, half of them with children. Mrs McGee, who lived in a 10 foot by 8 foot room with her six children, half of them under 10, had been deserted by her husband.

Only 12 of the households had any weekly income, ranging from 3d (1p) for Mrs Smith for sewing to 3s (15p) for Mrs Douglas, a winder, and Robert McNicol, a labourer. The monthly relief from the parish ranged from 2s 6d to 5s (12.5–25p). Temporary relief was 1s or 1s 6d (5p or 7.5p). Food, in the form of meal for making porridge, was given to almost every family, and as 20 had no beds or bedding, 12 straw beds were given.

It is hard to imagine, when we look at this evidence of poverty and hardship among the large number of Irish people who were then in Glasgow, that the situation could possibly get any worse – but the most severe famine in Irish history struck the country in the 1840s.

In 1845 the potato crop in Ireland was totally destroyed by a plant disease known as 'blight' and the period known as 'The Great Famine' began. The destruction of the crop took with it virtually the only means of avoiding starvation that had been left to the poor of Ireland. Handley says of the Irish labourer:

> Self improvement was the impulse which transported him to Scotland in pre-famine days. Self preservation was the urge which drove him onwards in the dark night of pestilence.

Now the Irish were forced to desert their country in their hundreds of thousands – that is, those who were capable of it – for while it is known that up to 1 million people emigrated from Ireland at this terrible time, it is believed that at least another million died from starvation and fever. The episode is one of great bitterness in Irish history. Historians argue that when the 'famine' was at its worst, between 1845 and 1847, it was not due to lack of food in the country, since millions of pounds worth of farm produce was exported to Britain during this time; rather, this was a famine of the poor, whose survival was dependent on the poor man's crop – potatoes. Eventually, the government set up the usual committees of enquiry and sent about £10 million in aid to Ireland, but it was too little, too late and the population was decimated by death and emigration.

Thousands of those who did escape now crowded on to the steamers that brought them to the Clyde; about 8,000 Irish people a week were arriving in Glasgow at the peak of the famine.

Many came to Scotland, and Glasgow in particular, simply because they could not afford the fare to America, and most of those who came to the city were on the verge of starvation when they landed. There was a panic that the city was going to be flooded out by hordes of ragged, starving beggars bringing disease with them. In 1848–9, when cholera was raging in the city, taking almost 4,000 lives alone in a four-month period, *The Annual Mortality Report* recorded that:

> in Glasgow, as well as in Edinburgh, there is of late a gradually increasing rate of mortality which may be fairly attributed to the increase of Irish immigration with its concomitant misery, destitution and pauperism. To check this growing evil, productive not only of increased death but of fearfully increased pecuniary burdens among our city population, is absolutely necessary, otherwise Glasgow will become a city of paupers and plague.

Two centuries of the 'misgovernment' had created a picture of the Irish as a race not far above slaves, an impression confirmed by the fact that the Scots saw the very poorest of the people as they landed in Scotland, in full flight from fever and starvation.

By the 1850s, the poverty of the masses in industrial Britain had led to changes in the Poor Law, and needy people were now investigated by inspectors in each parish whenever they applied for financial assistance. The volumes of the *Poor Relief Applications* in Glasgow City Parish contain an Irish Series, which contains hundreds of harrowing cases, including the following.

Charles McMahon had lost his left leg below the knee while working for the railway. His former employer had no responsibility for him, even though he had served his apprenticeship there and was now incapable of working.

Bridget O'Rourke, aged 14, a mill worker with an 'impaired mind', was destitute because she had injured her right hand in Mr McPhail's mill and was unfit for work. Mr McPhail had given her 5/- and the promise of her job back when she had recovered. Bridget would never recover because her hand was totally useless.

Another applicant asked for a coffin and ground in which to bury his baby: the second application – and the second baby.

Yet another destitute family was that of Mary McCavery Smith. Her

1841.   7, Water Street, Liverpool.

STEAM CONVEYANCE FOR BELFAST,
BY A FIRST-CLASS STEAM-SHIP.

The TARTAR,............Captain STEWART, IS INTENDED TO SAIL AS UNDER:—

FROM GLASGOW,	FROM BELFAST,
JULY. Vessel. Railway.	JULY.
Mon., 26th, at 3 P.M....6 P.M.	Wednesday, ...28th, at 6 P.M.
Friday, 30th, at 8 P.M.... ——	Monday, 2d August, at 9 P.M.

The TARTAR will remain at Greenock for the arrival of Passengers by the Railway Trains, which leave Glasgow at the hours noted above.

Cabin Passage, 10s., Fee, 2s.—Steerage, 2s. 6d.

Passengers are particularly requested to look after their own Personal Luggage, as the Proprietors will not be accountable for any article whatever, unless *entered and signed* for as received by them or their Agents.

For Freight or Passage, apply to Mr. Hill Charley, Belfast; Messrs. Kippen & Lindsay, Greenock; or here, to

THOMSON & MACCONNELL,
15, Jamaica Street.

Glasgow, July, 1841.

GLASGOW AND LONDONDERRY STEAMERS.

THE GLASGOW AND LONDONDERRY STEAM PACKET COMPANY'S Powerful and Fast-sailing STEAM VESSELS,

ROVER,.........................Capt. DAVID WYSE,
ST. COLUMB,... ....Capt. ALEX. COULTER,
FOYLE,........................Capt. JAS. TURNBULL,

Are intended to Sail in JULY—
FROM GLASGOW,

	By Railway Train to Greenock.
Rover,.........Monday, 26th July, at 5 Evening,	6 Evening.
St. Columb, Friday, 30th ... at 9 Morning.	12 Noon.

The ROVER calls at PORT-RUSH, and the ST. COLUMB at CAMPBELTON, both in going and returning.

Apply to John Lyon, Londonderry; J. Caldwell, Port-Rush; P. Watson, Campbelton; J. Martin, Greenock; and here, to

T. CAMERON & CO.,
7, Anderston Quay, Broomielaw.

Glasgow, July, 1841.

Advertisement in *The Glasgow Herald*, 26 July 1841.

husband had drowned at the Broomielaw but she had two children working in tobacco factories, one aged seven and earning 1/3d (6p) a week. Mary and her children were in a state of starvation and were being fed by their neighbours. The inspector granted her 1/6d (7.5p) temporarily while she made arrangements to go back to Ireland, possibly just to go and starve there instead. In 1849, the parish authorities in Scotland were sending people back to the Irish poorhouses at the rate of 1,000 people per month.

Many of those who had left Ireland in the hope of finding even a slightly better life in Glasgow were obliged, like Mary Smith, to put their small children to work in the mills and factories to bring home their share of money, however little this might have been. Many of these factories, in fact, depended heavily on the deft fingers and cheap labour provided by the children of immigrants.

Though some small improvement had taken place in earlier decades, by the 1860s the conditions for many children working in the factories and mills was causing concern, quite apart from the fact that most of these children were having no education. A commission set up to examine these conditions came to Glasgow to look at factories in the city. One such was a match factory in Duke Street, which employed many children. In this factory, 'one large room... is set apart entirely for young children, boys and girls' whose job it was to fill wooden frames with matches. One boy was Daniel McLachlad, aged 14, who told the investigators:

[that he had been] here two years. Hours are from 6 to 6. Stays sometimes till 7 or 7.30. Once till 9 or 10. That swelling (from ears to under the jaws) had been upon him these seven years... works by the piece; gets 3/- (15p) a week when there is plenty of work. Went to a week school once for a fortnight but left because he had to help his brother. Father and mother worked out.

First Report, Children's Employment Commission, 1863

People in the match industry suffered from a disease caused by the phosphorus in the matches, which rotted the teeth and jaws, and although there is no mention that this is Daniel's problem, some of the other children in the factory reported that they had seen it in other match factories. Many of these children had been working in the factory since they were seven or eight years old and most had no schooling, except perhaps attendance at the Sunday School, where they were taught to read the Bible.

The Poor Law Inquiries, the Poor Relief Applications and even the Children's Employment Investigations tell countless and almost unbelievable tales of what life was like for the poor Irish immigrants. It is somewhat surprising, then, to find that it soon became fashionable to accuse the Irish of coming to Scotland in their thousands in order to live off the sums of money provided by Poor Relief, which they were entitled to claim after three years' residence in Scotland. In 1858 the *Poor Law Magazine* began publication, and was very outspoken against the immigration of the Irish poor. One of those inspectors whose job was to help people in need wrote a poem for the magazine:

'The Irish Pauper in Ireland to his Neighbours'

Och! come from the West boys, come hook it with me;
'Tis a dirty ould peat bog polluting the sea,
Where black hunger grins from each mud cabin door;
Then come where there's parties and whisky galore.
They'll feed us, and clothe us, with all of the best,
And make us their own though we come from the West.
In the poorhouse of Scotland we'll live at our aise;
It's no more like our Unions than peats are like paise;
For here work and starvation is always the test,
Then why stay any longer in this Bog of the West?
But come from the West and in Scotland you'll find
Lots of grub, without work, and faith that's to your mind.

There is more of the poem, which suggests that the Scots are being taken for fools by these crafty Irish who have their families kept by charity, but the evidence suggests that the Irish poor, like the Scottish poor themselves, lived lives that were far from luxurious, even when they were in work. Wages, after all, were so low that when anything happened to interrupt their jobs these people quickly became destitute. Such was the case when the American Civil War cut off cotton supplies to Scotland in the 1860s. By this time many hundreds of immigrant women and children depended for their livelihoods on the numerous cotton mills in and around Glasgow. Out of work, the Irish had to depend on charity, bringing on themselves, as we have seen, a great deal of hostility. Besides this, the Irish came in for a lot of rough treatment in certain parts of Glasgow. A *Glasgow Herald* writer, known only as J. McN, reported:

About the year 1791 I mind of being over the water at Tradeston to see a famous itinerant who gave out prizes of fat sheep... at this show, two Irishmen, a rare thing, were discovered and a hunt after them immediately took place... and after they had been well thrashed by their gallant assailants, the triumph was celebrated by a drummer and fifer at the head of the mob.

'Hunting the Barney' was to become an annual demonstration against the Irish in Glasgow, particularly at the Glasgow Fair, when those caught were clubbed and beaten. It ended only when there were too many Irishmen in the city to take on.

Another method of abusing people who we resent is to make them into a joke. As with the Highlanders, the Irish also figured largely in cartoons, stories and comic songs. Songs like 'Barney Liggett' and the 'Connaught Man's Description of Glasgow' were sold in Glasgow in 1871:

I travelled the whole way from Donaghadee,
The flourishing city of Glasgow to see,
It's when I came there the first flesh meat I saw,
Was boiled roasted herrings at the Broomielaw.
Then oh! but it's pretty to live in the city
Where everything curious there is to be seen
The next place I came to was called the Exchange
Where three rows of buildings stood all in a range,
A large round square clock there was lighted with gas,
To let the blind people see the hours as they pass.
The next place I came to they called George Square,
A man on a high pillar was mounted there;
Two men for to guard them inside they did keep.
They stood winking at me tho' both fast asleep.
The next place I came to was called the Cross,
There I saw a blind man riding on a white horse,
His black thorn cudgel he was pointing straight,
Directing the lassies to the barrack gate.

The Irish were also nicknamed 'Patlanders' and were portrayed in newspapers and magazines as stupid, ignorant and dirty, besides being objects of suspicion. One writer commented,

Pat has to encounter sneers and gibes upon his drawl, his brogue, his very dress, air and manners, as well as upon his country and his religion.

Handley, The Irish in Scotland

But the Irish were here to stay, in spite of all the mockery and resentment, and better-informed people acknowledged that their labour was a valuable contribution to the industrial progress of the time. The Irish were prepared to tackle the heaviest of jobs, and there could have been few significant industrial developments in and around Glasgow that did not have their share of Irish effort in them. Road building, canals and railways all drew heavily on the existence of the Irish 'navvies' (the word, in fact, means 'navigator', and refers to the labourers who did the excavation work, or navigation, on these projects). In the 1890s the underground – the Glasgow Subway – was tunnelled and constructed largely by the use of Irish immigrant labour.

It would be wrong, of course, to suppose that all the Irish immigrants who came to Glasgow were factory workers or 'navvies', although these were by far the occupations of most. The heavy engineering projects, such as railway or canal building, relied heavily on Irish labourers, many of whom were recruited by advertisements in the Irish newspapers. A few of the Irish in Glasgow instead went into the second-hand clothes business – Paddy's Market for decades was a reminder of this particular kind of Irish enterprise – and some went into the entertainment world, appearing in music halls and theatres around Glasgow. Others, immigrants or the children of immigrants, were to contribute to the life of the city in other ways.

An interesting contrast with the usual image of the rough, illiterate Irish immigrant is John Lavery, a member of a highly respected group of artists, who became world famous as a portrait painter. An even better known son of Irish immigrants was Thomas Lipton, whose father, a poor labourer, had left Ireland at the time of the potato famine and had worked hard in a Glasgow mill until he had enough money to open a small grocer's shop. Born in a Glasgow tenement in 1850, Thomas was working in the shop by the time he was nine years old, and when he was 15 years old he emigrated to America, arriving there with 30s (£1.50) in his pocket. He worked on tobacco plantations in Virginia and in the rice fields of Carolina but was back in Glasgow by the time he was 20. On his 21st birthday, Lipton opened his first grocer's shop on Stobcross Street in Anderston, and by the age of 30 he was a millionaire. He owned

One of Lipton's grocer's shops.

a printing works and tea plantations in Ceylon, besides having a chain of shops in Glasgow and elsewhere. Perhaps it was as a result of his own family history, but Thomas Lipton was to be more than generous in sharing his wealth with the poor of Glasgow and when he died, unmarried, in 1931, he was to bequeath most of his great fortune to charities in the city.

There is not much evidence of Thomas Lipton's education, but if he was working in his father's shop at the age of nine then it suggests that he had little formal schooling. This was common for a time among Irish immigrants who had not come from a strong tradition of schooling for the poor. In Scotland, the idea that there should be some kind of education for everyone, however poor, had existed for a long time, even if the idea could not always be put into practice in a satisfactory way; but when the Irish did send their children to the parish schools in Glasgow they found, in any case, that the schools were run by Protestants

Thomas Lipton.

who saw it as their Christian duty to teach the Catholics the error of their ways and educate them away from their religion. The solution was for the Irish to set up their own schools and pay for them themselves, and the Catholic Schools Society was formed. The first of these schools were in areas where most of the Irish had settled, such as Bridgeton, the Gorbals and Anderston.

In 1872, when compulsory education was introduced in Scotland by Act of Parliament, the Catholic Church preserved the right to refuse state funding and continued to run and pay for their own schools with voluntary contributions from the Catholic population. This situation existed until 1918, when Catholic schools joined the others already in the state system, and were subsequently managed by Glasgow Corporation Education Authority. The 1918 Education (Scotland) Act, nevertheless, acknowledged the right of separate Catholic schools to maintain a programme of religious instruction and to select teachers.

By the beginning of the 20th century, Irish immigration to Scotland had been much reduced, but the numbers were to rise again when the First World War once again created a great need for labour in Britain as a whole, and by 1921 the census showed that there were 65,688 people of Irish birth in Glasgow. When we add the children born in this country to Irish immigrant parents, it is easy to see why the fear that the Irish were 'swamping' the native Scots refused to die out. The old discords were raised again when the war was over and jobs became hard to find.

To some extent, this title page speaks for itself, but inside the document there is a great deal of explanation of what the 'menace' consists of. It is most revealing that the Church of Scotland report identified the problem as resting in the twin sins of being Irish and Catholic. Scottish Catholics were excluded from the criticisms in the paper on the grounds that they were Scottish, and Irish Protestants in turn were acceptable because they were Protestants. The great fear expressed was that since so many Scots were now emigrating to America, or parts of the Empire, because of poor conditions at home, the Irish would be given an opportunity to 'take over'. The authors of the document, however, did not acknowledge that many of the 'Scots' who were emigrating were Highland or Irish in origin themselves.

The paper also suggested that Irish 'ghettos' were forming in cities such as Glasgow and Edinburgh, since 'respectable' people moved out when the Irish people invaded a district, to bring it down with their slovenly ways. It is odd, therefore, that the paper should also seem to contradict itself

The Menace of the Irish Race

to our Scottish Nationality

Be Scotland still to Scotland true
Amang oursels united!
For never but by Scottish hands
Maun Scottish wrangs be righted.
—*After Robert Burns.*

The Report to the General Assembly of the Church
of Scotland on the Irish Problem in Scotland. Notes
taken from Official Sources being added.

EDINBURGH

1923

A report to the Church of Scotland published in 1923,
The Menace of the Irish Race, shows that such animosity
and distrust could be made very public.

by claiming that the Irish were, on the one hand, lazy and irresponsible, and on the other, ambitious and wily. The writers claimed, after all, that the Irish, with

> ... their gift of speech, their aptitude for public life, their restless ambition to rule, have given them a prominent place.

The Irish did gain prominent positions in Glasgow life, in politics, business and other areas of public life, despite this open hostility or the less outspoken forms of discrimination that are believed to have operated against the Catholic Irish for many years, particularly in employment opportunities.

Today, there are many people in Glasgow who owe some part of their identity to an Irish immigrant background, even though they may no longer have any visible connection with their Irish origin. But there is

Like the Highlanders, (see Chapter 2) the Irish would often find accommodation only in the backlands.

Photograph by Thomas Annan.

also a significant number of Glaswegians with Irish origins who keep the contact alive through the language, music or dance of Ireland in clubs and associations. Such organisations are, in a sense, an acknowledgement of the fact that the movement of population between Ireland and Scotland has never ceased, as the 1991 Census records the presence of more than 10,000 people in Glasgow who were born in Ireland.

In the 2001 Census more than 15,000 people in Greater Glasgow identified themselves as Irish. This increase in number from 1991 may well lie in the fact that it was the first time the census in Scotland had included a question about ethnic identity.

Such a significant Irish presence in the city is well supported by the thriving Irish Gaelic scene in and around Glasgow. *Comhaltas Ceoltóiri Éireann* is an organisation dedicated to the promotion, performance and appreciation of traditional Irish music and culture. In 1957 the Glasgow Irish Minstrels was the first branch of *Comhaltas* to be formed outside Ireland. To date, the Irish Minstrels meet in St Roch's Secondary School and provide free tuition for lessons in all traditional musical instruments.

A notable date for the Glasgow Irish Minstrels was their 50th anniversary in January 2007. This was celebrated with a civic reception and ceilidh at the City Chambers and with a *Comhaltas* Young Traditionals concert during the Celtic Connections festival.

In the Pollok area of the city, another branch of *Comhaltas Ceoltóiri Éireann* meets in the church hall of St James the Great. The group welcomes an age range described as 'pre-5 to pensioners, and everything in between'. This branch was founded in 1989, by the then parish priest, and continues to thrive. Concerts and competitions at home and in Ireland keep the band busy. The branch website, however, stresses that 'the emphasis at St James has always been on teaching'. This is borne out by the fact that young members learn to play the whistle, flute, banjo, mandolin, fiddle, uilleann pipes, bodhran... the list goes on.

Yet another powerfully active Irish group in the city is the *Tir Connaill* Harps Gaelic Athletic Club. This club was set up in 1994, on the South Side of the city, and works extensively to introduce children to Gaelic team sports. The club has teams playing football, shinty and camogie (a close relative of hurling) and is serving a wide age range, from the Mini Harps to the various senior and ladies' teams. Between 1998 and 2006 the different teams and the individuals within them have collected many awards. The various teams also travel widely in Scotland and England, and frequently go to Ireland to compete in matches. The ladies' teams also took part in the Glasgow Women's Celtic Sports Festival in 2006, with participants invited from other clubs.

Tir Connaill Harps launched a new development plan in November 2006, and a guiding principle of the club is to make Gaelic sport as inclusive as possible: the club is active in, for example, school exchanges designed to 'promote religious and racial tolerance amongst young people'. In this work the club is supported by Glasgow City Council and Sense over Sectarianism, a Scottish Parliament-backed group that promotes inclusiveness and challenges sectarianism in Scottish society. Encouraging many non-Irish children to participate in Irish team sports, *Tir Connaill* Harps is playing a meaningful part in meeting this aim.

Croke Park.

As all of the above demonstrate, the Irish cultural and sporting areas of Glasgow are well served, but the arts and politics of the United Kingdom are also well represented by those of Irish descent. Too numerous to list, notable Scots of Irish descent include John Reid, formerly a Labour MP and Home Secretary in the Blair government; Tommy Sheridan, Glasgow-born leader of the new Socialist party Solidarity; and, of course, world-famous comedian Billy Connolly, born in the city in 1942, whose father, William, was the son of Irish immigrants. Bernard MacLaverty, also born in 1942, is a highly respected writer of novels and films and has made Glasgow his home for many years.

The Irish connection in the city is also underlined by the Irish presence on the board of *An Lòchran*, the Gaelic Arts Strategy body. This strategy looks forward to the flourishing of all aspects of Gaelic culture, both Scots and Irish, in the near future, and the board includes a representative of Irish interests, who is also vice-chair of *Comhaltas Ceoltóiri Éireann*.

It is hardly surprising, then, given the long history of the Irish in Glasgow, that Caledonian University's 2001 study showed that no less than half of the population of Glasgow have Irish or Scottish Gaelic in their recent family background.

Postscript 2016

On 27 March 2016, some 3,700 military personnel paraded through the streets of Dublin to commemorate the centenary of the Easter Rising in 1916. And in acknowledgement of a Scottish involvement, 'The 1916 Rising Centenary Committee (Scotland) was set up also in 2016, to remember those 'who sacrificed much in pursuit of an Irish Republic'.

The Rising was an armed insurrection, aiming to overthrow British Rule and establish an independent Irish Republic. It was to be the most significant armed uprising in Ireland since 1798.

Organised by a seven man Military Council of the Irish Republican Brotherhood, the Rising began on Easter Monday, 24 April 1916, and lasted for six days. Members of the Irish Volunteers, led by Patrick Pearse, together with the smaller Citizen's army of James Connolly and *Cumann na mBan* seized key locations in Dublin and proclaimed an Irish Republic.

The British Army responded by bringing in thousands of reinforcements and heavy artillery, and there were fierce battles in the streets of the city centre. The rebels put up stiff resistance, slowing the British advance and inflicting severe casualties.

By sheer force of numbers and more sophisticated weaponry the British Army suppressed the uprising and Patrick Pearse agreed to an unconditional surrender on Saturday 29 April. After courts-martial, 15 men identified as leaders were executed by firing squad in Kilmainham Jail, Dublin, including James Connolly. In all, 485 people were killed in the rebellion.

The Rising and the British reaction to it brought about increased support for Irish Independence, and in December 1918, republicans, represented by the Sinn Féin party, won a landslide victory in the General Election. Refusing to take their seats in Westminster, instead they convened the first Irish Parliament, the Dail, in Dublin. This led in 1921 to the Anglo Irish Treaty and the founding of the Irish Free State in 1922. The six counties of Ulster remained part of the United Kingdom.

Less well known is the role played in the rebellion by the Irish diaspora. It is now recognised that anywhere between 30 and 50 men and women based in Glasgow took part in the fighting during that Easter week, including a socialist from Denny, Charles Carrigan, who was killed in the evacuation of the General Post Office in O'Connell Street. Considerably more were active in Glasgow itself working, legally or otherwise, for the Irish cause.

A new major study, *Scotland and the Easter Rising*, published in 2016, and edited by Professor Willy Maley and Kirsty Lusk, features contributions from a range of writers, journalists and academics, reflecting the part played by Scotland in the rebellion, and its many legacies.

Central to the book is the story of James Connolly, born in Edinburgh to Irish immigrant parents, Commandant General of the Irish forces during that Easter week and a signatory to the Proclamation of the Irish Republic. Margaret Skinnider, a schoolteacher and suffragette born in Coatbridge, is another republican sympathiser who figures largely in the book. She served as scout, despatch rider, sniper and raider in the Rising and was the only female combatant injured in action.

In this seminal study of the role of Scots and Scots Irish in those events, Professor Maley writes:

> There has been very little proper acknowledgement of James Connolly's Scottishness, neither has much been written about the life of Margaret Skinnider and so many like her who hailed from Scotland and felt the need to join the Rising.

This collection of writings by no less than 28 Scottish and Irish writers of repute will stand as a valuable contribution to redressing that balance.

CHAPTER 4

Glasgow Jewry

NOT JUST THE Highlanders and the Irish were attracted to Glasgow at the beginning of the 19th century; the first recorded mention of a Jewish person in the city is on a 'burgess certificate', awarded to Isaac Cohen on 12 September 1812. He may have come to Glasgow from Edinburgh, as there is known to have been a small Jewish community there from the 1780s. Isaac Cohen was a hatter to trade, and was later to be described as 'the man who introduced the silk hat to Scotland'. Before he could pursue his trade in Glasgow, however, Isaac required a burgess certificate. Only men who had this privilege were allowed to trade in the city. This certificate served two purposes in that it reduced the possibility of too much competition but it was also intended to exclude anyone who was not a member of the official church. Anyone taking the oath for the certificate had to promise to uphold the 'true religion' and renounce Roman Catholicism. Isaac was willing to make this declaration even though he was a Jew, but he must have found it difficult to practise his own religion, as he appears to have been the only Jew in the city.

> Here I protest before God that I confess and allow with my heart the true **Religion** presently professed within this Realm and authorised by the laws thereof. I shall abide thereat and defend the same to my Life's end, renouncing the Roman Religion called Papistry. I shall be leal and true to our **Sovereign Lord the King's Majesty** and to the Provost and Baillies of this 'Burgh.

At that time, Isaac was probably quite pleased to be able to set up in business in Glasgow because as a Jew he would have suffered many disadvantages in other parts of the world. From time immemorial it had been the lot of the Jews to be in the minority in the lands in which they travelled or settled. These were other 'nations' with other religions and traditions. Jews had no 'homeland' of their own from 70AD until the founding of the state of Israel in 1948. For centuries it had fallen to the Jews to be discriminated against, and cruelly persecuted for their faith and traditions. Jews were to be found in all the cities of Europe, often restricted to living in a part of the city specially set aside for them, known as a 'ghetto'.

The term 'ghetto' originated in Venice in the 1500s. It meant 'foundry'. In Venice, the Jews were sent to live in the area of Ghetto Nuovo (or New Foundry), an area surrounded by high walls and with gates manned by Christian guards who locked the Jews inside at night. Gradually, the word 'ghetto' came to mean the Jewish quarter, but today the term is commonly used to describe any area in which people are forced to live, either through their circumstances or by the authorities.

The earliest Jews in Glasgow were not, on the whole, poor refugees who came to Scotland to escape persecution – these were to come later; rather, they were businessmen or merchants, mainly of German or Dutch origin, who preferred to leave Europe because of the insecure conditions caused by the Napoleonic Wars. By 1823 there were enough of them in Glasgow to worship together and the first synagogue in Glasgow was a 'room and kitchen' in High Street, inhabited by Moses Lisenheim and his wife. Among the other leaders of the tiny Jewish community in the city were David Davies, an instrument maker, and a furrier named Levy. From announcements he paid for in the *Glasgow Chronicle* and the *Glasgow Directory* between January 1817 and 1824 (see page 60) we know that Mr P. Levy was practising his trade as a furrier in Hutcheson Street.

In 1831, James Cleland was to include 47 Jews in his census of the population of Glasgow. Some of this number were to raise the 100 guineas (£105) that were needed to purchase a small part of the new cemetery just opened beside the cathedral – the Necropolis. Before this time, since there was no Jewish burial ground in Glasgow, and when there were no railways, the Jews of Glasgow had to suffer the distressing experience of carrying the bodies of their dead relatives to bury them in Edinburgh.

The new cemetery in Glasgow was soon in use, since cholera was making one of its frequent appearances in the city, and the first recorded burial in the cemetery was that of Joseph Levi, who died of cholera.

On 1 March 1894, J. S. Rubenstein, writing from London to the *Evening Citizen*, described some of his boyhood experiences in Glasgow in those early days of the Jewish community:

I had an uncle living or travelling about in Scotland intending to settle there. He wrote for his wife to come and join him in Glasgow. We lived in Russia and my age was then 11 years. My parents were afraid I'd be taken for a Russian Soldier. He encouraged her to go to her husband and as it would not have been proper for a lady to travel alone I was sent as her escort. We came to Glasgow on 20 August 1829. We wrote we were coming so we were sent to Guildry Court, Bridgegate... When the man Levi died in the year of the cholera (1832) the arrangements for his burial were made by two men and a boy. I was the boy. We put in the coffin lots of lime and plenty of water before we screwed it down. No-one else attended because there were so few Jews in Glasgow and some had to attend to their business while the rest were afraid of the cholera. Mr Crown, with myself, had to watch the grave one night out of seven to prevent thieves getting up the bodies and selling them to the doctor. I left your country about 1834 went to Ireland and lived in Dublin for 25 years.

Evening Citizen, 1 March 1894

This particular boy did not stay in Glasgow very long, but most of the Jews who came did seem to stay and the number grew steadily, if not dramatically. By 1850, it was estimated that there were about 200 Jews in Glasgow, and a new synagogue had been set up in a back-court building in Candleriggs. Some of the community were becoming quite prosperous, and were willing to extend financial help to those Jews who were less fortunate, a traditional feature of Jewish society. When Asher Asher, born in 1837 to a poor Jewish family in Glasgow, showed promise as a scholar, other Jews paid for him to be trained as a doctor at Glasgow University. Asher Asher became the first Jewish student at the university and the first Jewish physician to qualify there.

By the time Asher Asher went to university, many of the restrictions that had been placed upon the Jews, both in Scotland and England, had been removed by law. From 1828, the Jews of England had been struggling for the civil and political emancipation that the Roman Catholics achieved in 1829, but it was not until 1835 that Jews were allowed to vote in elections or hold public office. They could not attend the ancient universities until 1853, and did not become full citizens of the country until 1858.

In other countries of Europe, however, where millions of Jews lived, the reverse of this British legal process was true and the persecution and expulsion of Jewish communities in various parts of Europe was to continue throughout most of this period. As a result, Jews were to emigrate in their millions from Europe to almost anywhere else in the world.

It is believed that in the Middle Ages 80 per cent of all the Jews in the world lived in Poland. However, several times throughout the 18th

POSITIVELY THE LAST WEEK'S SALE
OF THAT
EXTENSIVE STOCK OF FURS
At No. 90,
HUTCHESON STREET,
BY P. LEVY,
THE ONLY FUR MANUFACTURER IN SCOTLAND
Great Bargains may be Expected.

Mr P. Levy, furrier, advertising his business in the *Glasgow Chronicle*,
January 1817 and Directory of 1824–6.

century, parts of Poland, which included huge numbers of Polish and
Lithuanian Jews, were brought under Russian rule. The Jews were to
become the second largest ethnic minority in Russia, outnumbered only
by the Poles themselves. The Russian authorities – **both** church and state
– feared that the Jews would 'contaminate' the Russian population – but
probably feared Jewish economic competition even more – **and** adopted
legal discrimination against the Jews, restricting them to the Pale of
Settlement, which has been described as 'a super ghetto, stretching from
the Baltic to the Black Sea'. Millions of Jews living in the Pale were treated
as second-class citizens in matters of education and the professions.
Worse still, fathers and mothers sometimes had to stand by and watch
helplessly while their young sons were dragged off to serve in the Russian
army for up to 31 years. From 1827 until 1859, when the practice was
stopped, tens of thousands of boys over the age of 12 were taken into the
Russian army. (J. S. Rubenstein's parents had sent him away to Glasgow
with his aunt because they were afraid this would happen to him when
he was 12.)

Even within the Pale, laws were passed that restricted the Jews to living
and working in the towns, so that they seldom became landowners or
farmers but learned instead the skills of trade or commerce, becoming
pedlars, tailors, butchers, and so on. Jews needed skills that could quickly

be transplanted elsewhere when the persecution reached the intolerable levels of the frequent pogroms, when Jews were beaten, starved and expelled from their homes.

This level of violence reached a new peak after 1881, when the Jews were blamed for the assassination of the Russian Czar, Alexander II. Massive expulsions of Jews took place and people simply fled to wherever they might be able to survive. The restrictions had often meant that the Jews lived in poverty in congested conditions in the ghettos, and millions of them were prepared to settle for very little to find a place where they could live in reasonable freedom. Between 1881 and 1930 it is believed that no less than four million Jews left Eastern Europe, mostly for America, but some to Canada, Australia or Palestine. Many Jews had to pass through Britain on the way to America and reached no further. Over 200,000 Jewish people came to Britain and settled during this period, several thousand of them in Glasgow. Some of those who arrived in Glasgow in the 1880s came from England but many others landed on the east coast of Scotland, or in Greenock – some believed that they had already reached America.

Most of the 600 or 700 Jews who were already settled in the city lived on the north side of the river, and the large Garnethill Synagogue, built to serve this substantial congregation in 1879, was then the centre of Jewish life in Glasgow. But the new arrivals were poorer people who could not afford to look for homes on the north side of the city. Instead,

> destitute, distraught and often dirty they packed into slums that
> the British and even the Irish were trying to quit.
>
> Huxley, *Back Streets: New Worlds*

These Jewish refugees from Russia and Poland now flocked into the Gorbals, where they settled down and practised those few occupations, mainly street trading and tailoring, which had been permitted to them in the ghettos of Eastern Europe. In fact, so many of the Jews who came to Glasgow were tailors that when the first synagogue was opened in the South Side, in Commerce Street, it was known as 'The Tailors' Synagogue'.

Traditionally, a Jewish community looks after the welfare of its less fortunate members, and the influx of poor Jews from Eastern Europe must have made heavy demands on the Jewish charities in Glasgow. In 1858 the Glasgow Hebrew Philanthropic Society had been set up to provide weekly pensions and grants to the sick and needy – and the Ladies' Society distributed food and clothes where these were needed. But the persecution of the Jews still in Russia was to continue with such a vengeance that their rescue and welfare was to become a matter of concern for all reasonable people, and a Distress Fund was set up in Britain in 1891. This was a cause that united all kinds of people in condemnation of such persecution and the Glasgow Fund had many non-Jewish contributors.

PERSECUTION OF THE JEWS OF RUSSIA

A public meeting of citizens was held in the Merchants' Hall yesterday, in terms of an influential requisition addressed to the Hon, the Lord Provost, for the purpose of raising funds, in co-operation with London and other cities in the United Kingdom, for the relief of the distressed, expelled Jews of Russia. Considering the hour of meeting and the inclemency of the weather, there was a good attendance. The chair was occupied by Baillie Cumming, in the absence of the Lord Provost from indisposition. Amongst the gentleman on the platform were: Sir Michael Connal, Archbishop Eyre; Mr J. G. A. Baird, MP; Mr John Wilson, MP; Councillors Fife, Mason, Dicksen, Sinclair, Macfarlane, and Mayberry; Principal Douglas, Bishop Harrison, Rev. Dr Donald Macleod, Rev. Dr Kerr, Rev. William Paterson, Rev. W Forrest, Messrs J. C. White of Overtoun, W. A Campbell, J. S. Morris, H. A. Long, Barclay, J. Frankenborg, Alexander Lamberton, D. M. Scott, Messrs Buchanan, W. G. Black, J. Piate, &c.

Glasgow Herald, 23 January 1892

Jewish emigration from Europe often took the form of the father emigrating first, and later sending for his wife and family when he had work and a place to live. In 1901, the Glasgow Hebrew Benevolent Society was founded to help these Jewish immigrants to set up in business. Money would be loaned to buy, for example, pedlar's stock. Even so, it was always the objective of any Jewish welfare organisation to 'promote self respect and independence among the recipients of help'. Glasgow Jews point out that few Jews ever had to depend on Parish Poor Relief of the kind grudgingly given to the native poor, or the Irish. The accusation that poor Jewish immigrants were a burden on the rates was simply untrue in Glasgow. Such an accusation was part of a campaign that resulted in legislation to control the flow of immigrants from Eastern Europe. The Aliens Order of 1905 was to affect people who did not have British citizenship coming to, or living in, Britain for many years to come, including during the two world wars.

One family was typical of many Jewish immigrants of this time. A young immigrant from Kamenets – Podolsk came to Glasgow in 1903 and found work as a joiner and cabinetmaker in the city. In 1906 he sent for his wife, his young son and his sister Golda, who was then 20 years of age. Golda, her sister-in-law and her nephew left Ukraine during the pogroms of 1905–6.

By 1914, and the outbreak of the First World War, all aliens in Glasgow had to register with the police, who proposed to intern or deport them if they had come from what were now enemy countries. The Jewish Representative Council, however, which had been set up in 1914, guaranteed the conduct of all such Jews in Glasgow and this was accepted by the authorities.

Golda was to settle down in the Gorbals, and would marry and live in Glasgow for the rest of her life, but in all that time she never became a British citizen and so was required to register with the police, since she was in law regarded as a foreigner. This was particularly true in wartime, and it is apparent from these extracts from Golda's registration card that she was required to

From the *Glasgow Herald*, 23 April 1892. This is the fifth list of subscriptions to the Russian Jews Distress Fund. Listed in old, pre-decimal money, it shows that in the three months Glasgow had raised a total of £4708-2s-2d. This is the equivalent of £201,130.46 raised today.

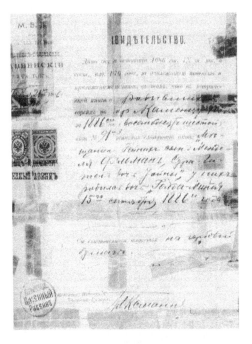

Golda Felman's birth certificate (above) and ID card (below).

report her movements to the police, and needed their permission to be out of the house between the hours of 10.30 p.m. and 6 a.m. What this really meant is brought home to us when we realise that on one occasion Golda was obliged to ask permission to visit Adelphi Street during those hours. It is difficult to come to terms with police permission to go 'first-footing'.

Golda's registration book shows that she was required to register until at least 1961, and it would appear that, although she could speak English, she had not learned to write the language in all that time, because in 1940, when she had been 24 years in Glasgow, she was still signing her card with a thumb print, the alternative to writing her name in English.

The English language and the Jewish religion were two of the initial problems facing children in the schools of Glasgow. By 1885 more than half the pupils in Gorbals Primary were Jewish, and they had to have their Hebrew lessons and prayers separately from the other children. In 1895, however, the first proper religious school was opened, the Talmud Torah, which the Jewish children attended *after* day school, something they were not terribly keen to do!

The immigrant Jew lived a fairly self-contained and independent existence in Glasgow – well organised but poor, tolerated but not quite accepted. Sometimes, it was simply the foreign appearance of the earliest immigrants which led to them being treated with some suspicion, if nothing worse. In a book about the city written in 1893, the author, describing several 'foreigners' he meets during a stroll in Kelvingrove Park, says of one:

> A glance at him is sufficient to proclaim him a son of Israel. He is a moneylender in the city – like not a few of his tribe – and his conversation has reference no doubt, to some advantageous bond he has received.
>
> Hammerton, *Sketches from Glasgow*

Most people who criticised the Jews, however, did so in less fancy language. Instead, the Scots criticised them for working and trading on Sundays, and the unions were concerned about cheap immigrant labour affecting the conditions of other workers. It was also said that it was difficult to rent a house if you were a Jew, but that would be harder to prove, except in those places where the landlords put up 'No Jews' signs. In any case, there was no shortage of Jews who managed to get houses in the Gorbals, but perhaps that simply confirms that they found it difficult to get houses anywhere else. It is more attractive to think that the Jewish immigrants gravitated to the Gorbals to be among friends and to enjoy the rich and colourful atmosphere of synagogue, *kosher* butcher and the Yiddish language, which was spoken by most of the immigrants.

But gradually, a new generation of Jews was being born in Glasgow, who were in contact with a culture that was not that of their parents. The new generation was losing the Yiddish language of their parents, and in an attempt to keep the language alive in Scotland, the first Jewish newspaper was born in Glasgow. This was the *Jewish Times*, published from 1903, followed by *The Jewish Voice*, a monthly paper published in Yiddish, first printed in August 1914. The joint owner of the paper was Mr Zevi Golombok who, with his brother, had left Lithuania in 1905 when that country was under Russian control. Neither Zevi nor his brother spoke any English, but that did not deter the two young men from setting themselves up as printers. They printed their first Yiddish newspaper just as the First World War broke out, an unfortunate time for any venture. A lasting monument to the Golombok brothers and their

The 'masthead' of the first *Jewish Echo*, published in January 1928.

enterprise was to be the *Jewish Echo*, founded in 1928 and published weekly until its closure in May 1992.

In all that time, the newspaper was an invaluable asset to the Jewish people, keeping them in touch with Jewish news – local, national and international – the 'flag', in a sense, of the Jewish community in Glasgow. In July 1993, Dr Ezra Golombok, editor of the newspaper and son of its founder, donated to the Mitchell Library a complete publication set of the *Jewish Echo*, covering its 64 years of existence. When the paper ceased publication in its Eglinton Street premises in 1992, it ended another long association of Jewish life with the Gorbals area of Glasgow.

This memorial has pride of place in the Synagogue of Garnethill *British Jewry Book of Honour, 1914–18.*

In its heyday, the Gorbals community supported five main synagogues, such as the Great Central Synagogue in South Portland Street (1901–74) as well as a number of smaller ones. Soon, a considerable number of social organisations were also to emerge: the Jewish Institute, a social club for the community, began in 1900, and other social and recreational clubs for young people followed and were very popular. Particularly popular was the Jewish football team, the Oxford Star, which was obliged to disband when the war began. But perhaps the most interesting example of the Jewish–Scottish cultural mix was the Jewish Lads' Brigade, founded in Glasgow in the 1900s and boasting the only all-Jewish pipe band in the world. Kilted Jews were, however, to become a more familiar sight during the two world wars, when young Jews took their place alongside Scots of all creeds in the various Scottish regiments.

In the years following the First World War, society gradually settled down, and the Jews of Glasgow worked on to establish themselves and their families. They did not all succeed; many were poor, but by 1935 a Jewish writer was describing the changes he sees from the early days when:

they were pedlars, tailors, one man shopkeepers... grubbing a hard life but patiently enduring with the synagogue behind them... in those days they were an inseparable element from the Barrows... they did not boast stalls, only barrows; barrows piled high with old clothes, old china cups and ornaments... cheaps and seconds.

This is only one example of the many hundreds of pictures and thousands of names which fill the pages of the *British Jewry Book of Honour* from the First World War. The soldiers are brothers H. and J. Finn of the Seaforth Highlanders, the girl possibly their sister. *British Jewry Book of Honour, 1914–18.*

Jewish Chronicle, July 1935

But by the time of writing the Glasgow Jews had large, successful businesses while their sons were doctors, lawyers or teachers, and 'speak with a Kelvinside accent'. And indeed, the *Jewish Echo* recorded the appointment of the first two Jewish teachers in Gorbals School in 1928.

GORBALS PUBLIC SCHOOL

Two Jewish Teachers Appointed

For the first time in the history of Gorbals School, Jewish teachers have been added to the staff. Miss Dora Stelmach, MA, and Mr J. Bernstein, BSC, AIC, both of whom are well-known locally, commenced duties this week. Both were at one time pupils of this school. It is a well-known fact that a majority of the pupils of Gorbals School are Jewish but whether any significance may be attached to the appointment of Jewish teachers it is difficult to say. There was a movement on foot some years ago to convert Gorbals school into a Jewish school where the teaching of Hebrew etc., would be added to the curriculum. We understand that one of the main reasons for the failure of this project was an insistence that no other Hebrew instruction be given. Since the short time which would have been devoted to such instruction during ordinary school hours would hardly be sufficient, the whole scheme was allowed to drop.

Jewish Echo, 5 October 1928

By the 1930s, some Jews were moving out of the Gorbals and into the more prosperous suburbs further south, but Jewish life for the most part still centred on the Gorbals. The same commentator, who wrote in the *Jewish Chronicle*, was English and he expressed his surprise about the lifestyle of those Jews who still lived in the Gorbals tenements:

the horror of Glasgow grows on one... the whole city is composed of three and four-storey tenements, all built in depressing grey and ochre granite... it is in such a city that 15,000 Jews have made their home. To the Jews of Hackney and Hampstead it may seem strange that fellow Jews should elect to live in such a drab domicile... where the children can have little freedom, and where the entry is through a series of dirty, gloomy passages and up endless flights of stairs. Yet thousands of Jews live in these tenements apparently content with their lot.

But, perhaps the Jews of the Gorbals were reasonably content with their lot because, as Paul Vincent wrote in 1982:

here the Rule of Law took precedence over the whims of local rulers... [Jews]... living side by side in Gorbals with Highlanders who had been forced out of their crofts and the Irish who had been starved out of their patches of land, relations between the three cultures were almost invariably good at the individual level.

Kaplan and Hutt, *A Scottish Shtetl*

A Scottish Shtetl was published by the Gorbals Fair Society to mark an exhibition of Jewish history and culture in Glasgow. The booklet dealt with Jewish life in the Gorbals between 1880 and 1974 – a *shtetl is* a Jewish community. In its pages some of the older people recorded their memories of a Jewish childhood in the Gorbals:

On Sunday morning the men stood at Gorbals Cross, they also chatted in Yiddish... on the other side there were the Irish immigrants, but they got on together all right.

And the Jewish children would play in the street: I remember when we used to play and make a noise outside a certain woman's window, she would open the window and shout out in her broken English – 'Get away or I'll make you black and red' – and we would shout up – 'You mean black and blue, Mrs Cohen' – and she would say – 'Don't bother me mit colours.'

Kaplan and Hutt, *A Scottish Shtetl*

'Cohen' is quite a common Jewish name, but in Glasgow it seemed to become more common than ever if the following is anything to judge by. Evelyn Cowan, in her autobiography, *Spring Remembered*, tells of how her father arrived at Greenock in 1900, and, unable to pronounce his name clearly enough for the immigration officials, was told 'Be Cohen like the rest of them'. Evelyn's father did not care for the name and changed it to Cowan. In her book, Evelyn Cowan describes the close-knit community that the Gorbals was in her childhood – the synagogues, meeting places, dance halls, Jewish food shops – and the survival of many Jewish customs brought from Eastern Europe. In 1974 Evelyn Cowan looks at the Gorbals with nostalgia for the 1930s.

For the Jews of Europe, however, the 1930s was not a happy time. The skies darkened once again for Jews, and anti-Semitic practices, never totally eliminated, rose to the surface again in several parts of Europe. In the 1920s and 1930s much of Europe was experiencing a period of

GORBALS CROSS SUNDAY MORNING

Gorbals Cross, before the redevelopment of the Gorbals in the latter part
of the 20th century.

economic depression, with mass unemployment, high inflation and all the associated hardships. At such times, people feel insecure and look for an outlet for their resentment. As in times past, the Jews were there to be scapegoats. For several years, the *Jewish Echo* reported the build-up of malice and violence towards their fellow Jews on the Continent.

'KILL THE JEWS AND SAVE RUSSIA'

Anti-Semite sent to mental hospital for attacking Jews

Moscow – For shouting the old cry of the Russian anti-Semites, 'Kill the Jews and save Russia' and attacking the family of a Jewish religious teacher (Melamed) in Penza, in European East Russia, an anti-Semite named Frolov has been sentenced to detention in a mental hospital instead of imprisonment. The Court found that Frolov had been guilty only of hooliganism and not of anti-Semitism. The population is angry at the decision and the local paper demands a retrial.

ANTISEMITIC CLERGYMEN IN GERMANY OBJECT TO FINANCING OF MISSIONARY WORK AMONG JEWS

Berlin – A protest against the decision of the Prussian General Synod to compel the collection of donations for the purpose of conducting missionary work among Jews was made by a number of anti-Semitic clergymen in Prussia. The protest is also directed against the order of the Synod compelling the clergy to offer special prayers for the success of the conversions among Jews.

ANTISEMITES TRYING TO CREATE UNITED FRONT OF CATHOLICS AND PROTESTANTS AGAINST THE JEWS IN GERMANY

Berlin – A united front of Catholics and Protestants for the purpose of fighting the Jews is planned in Germany, according to an announcement made today by the notorious anti-Semitic leader, Adolph Hitler, in addressing a Convention in Munich, of the Bavarian Hitlerist group.

'We shall never rest until the Jewish problem is settled,' Hitler stated in the course of his address.

CHILDREN PLAYING TRUANT FROM SCHOOLS IN GERMANY SPREAD STORIES THAT THEY WERE KIDNAPPED BY JEWS IN BLACK MOTOR-CARS WHO THREATENED TO KILL THEM

Berlin – Terrible stories about Jews carrying off Christian children in order to kill them have been spread about in a large number of places in Upper Silesia. The children have been telling stories about being kidnapped by Jews with long earlocks who came rushing up in a black motor-car. The anti-Semitic Press reprinted these stories as evidence given by children and worked up a frightful anti-Jewish agitation.

The Central Union of German Citizens of the Jewish Faith has investigated the stories and has established that the stories were invented by the children, who had been playing truant from school and had hit on this way of escaping punishment.

Jewish Echo, 1928

Once again in Europe, the mass movements of Jews began, and between 1933 and 1939 hundreds of thousands of German and Austrian Jews left their homelands.

They fled to all corners of the world, from Shanghai to South America, scattered like leaves before a storm.

Walvin, *Passage to Britain*

Of those Jews who stayed, no less than six million died in the horror camps of the Nazi Holocaust. Among those who escaped, some 60,000 came to Britain, where various organisations had been set up to help them. In Glasgow the Jewish orphanage, the Gertrude Jacobson, was already caring for German children by 1935. In 1939 a hostel for refugees was also opened in Garnethill and fundraising for this new generation of persecuted Jews was begun.

For those who came to Glasgow, perhaps the warmest reception in the city was to be found at 'Geneen's'. This was the name of a hotel and then a restaurant run by Mrs Sophie Geneen. The lasting power of her personality – the Jewish people of the city remember her as the 'Mother of Glasgow' – is shown in this memory of her by her daughter:

I remember Mama, as if I could ever forget this woman, so full of warmth, strength and sincerity and whose greatest pleasure was to give to all humanity those in need, hungry, cold or just lonely... no-one was ever turned away.

Kaplan and Hutt, *A Scottish Shtetl*

With war fast approaching and the treatment of the Jews steadily worsening, the Jews of Glasgow were anxious to play their part in alleviating the suffering where they could. In December 1938, a group of children, victims of the Nazi pogrom, arrived to be fostered in homes in the city. There were only a dozen children but literally hundreds of people turned out to meet them.

For three hours Glasgow Jews who had promised homes for Jewish refugee children from Germany waited the arrival of a party of 12 boys and girls in the Central Station... Several hundred members of the Jewish community in Glasgow were at the station to meet the children.

Glasgow Herald, 23 December 1938

While most people were appalled by what was happening again to the Jews, there were some voices quite close to home that seemed to have little sympathy for their plight. In a speech on the 'Jewish Problem', the Rev. James Black, a Church of Scotland minister, argued that:

[t]here are only two ways to treat the Jews, and these are either to fight them or convert them. Britain's desire is not to fight them but to see them converted to accepting the pure and unsophisticated principles of the Christian religion as their faith. Herr Hitler is only imitating others and his methods have done no good... The problem which the Jews present is that they have a presence among other nationalities of a race of people with no land of their own who still wish to preserve their racial identity and remain unassimilated with the people amongst whom they dwell.

Glasgow Herald, 10 March 1938

The Rev. Black presumed to speak for the entire country when he asserted that the conversion of the Jews was desirable, but there was very little evidence of this in Glasgow at least. At this time, there were certainly several anti-Semitic incidents in Glasgow but they were the exception rather than the rule.

SWASTIKAS SCRATCHED ON WINDOWS

Malicious damage was done to a number of Jewish shops in Glasgow and extensive anti-Jewish propaganda appeared in Jewish-owned property during the black-out at the weekend. About 20 windows or glass panels were cracked and swastikas were scratched with a diamond or metal tool on nearly 80 others.

The discovery of the majority of these destructive acts was made on Monday morning and the police were engaged in pursuing enquiries throughout the day.

Most of the shops affected are situated in Sauchiehall Street, though shops in Argyle Street and Stockwell Street were also damaged. Women's dress shops, furriers and tailors suffered most. A few of the windows had the words, 'We don't want Jews' printed on the glass, but not all the shops affected are Jewish-owned.

Jewish Echo, November 1939

The Jews themselves felt, for the most part, that Glasgow was not such a bad place to live. Certainly, in the more affluent parts of the city there tended to be discrimination in golf, bowling or tennis club membership, but it was the same city which agreed to boycott German goods in 1933 because of that country's treatment of its Jews. The Jewish leader, Rev. Cosgrove, was later to say that in spite of the slums and dreadful social problems of the city, 'Glasgow was a much pleasanter place for Jews to live than most others in Europe'.

As a response to what was happening to their fellow Jews in Europe, however, some Glasgow Jews decided to emigrate to Palestine to work for the permanent Jewish homeland that had been promised to the Jews of the world.

The Zionist movement for the setting up of a Jewish homeland began in 1897. The movement was active in Glasgow for many years; the first Zionist Association in the city was founded in 1898. Notwithstanding the organisation's real objective – the achievement of a Jewish home in Palestine – the Glasgow branch acknowledged the Scottish connection in its banner – a Star of David enclosed in the centre of a Scottish Lion Rampant. The treatment of the Jews of Europe once again led to the refounding of the Glasgow Zionist Association in 1928, and a significant number were drawn to emigrate to Palestine.

A sadder image of Geneen's restaurant records the passing of the Gorbals these people knew, but Sophie Geneen will never be forgotten since her memory lives on in the forest in Israel that bears her name.

SRC Archives.

A GLASGOW ZIONIST AND A NEW SYNAGOGUE IN TEL AVIV

The Foundation Stone was laid on the 15th of Shebat of a Synagogue in Bayit Vegan, a new suburb of Tel Aviv. The convener of the Building Committee is Mr I. Glass, a prominent Glasgow Zionist, who settled in Eretz Yisrael some time ago, having purchased a share in the Bayit Vegan scheme. There are a number of other Glasgow Zionists who are interested in this new settlement, which is near Tel Aviv. Thirty houses are already built there.

Jewish Echo, 2 March 1928

The Jewish homeland, the State of Israel, was formally set up in 1948 and ever since then a steady trickle of Glasgow Jews, particularly young people, have left to make their homes there.

Glasgow Jews, nevertheless, were sufficiently Glaswegian to become involved in the politics of city or country. Just as thousands of Jews fought for their country in two world wars, so did a smaller group of men fight for the conditions of all the people in the field of politics. Best known among them is the Red Clydesider, Emmanuel Shinwell, who served Labour politics for many, many years. 'Manny', who died on 8 May 1986 aged 101 years, acknowledged that he was not a true Glasgow man – he was born in London – but he spent a very large part of his life in and around Glasgow working for ordinary people of all creeds.

'Manny' Shinwell is probably the best-known Glasgow Jew today, but there have been, and still are, many Jews who have brought credit to the city, such as the first Jewish Lord Provost, Sir Myer Galpern, who died in 1993. There are also those out of the public gaze, working in the professions or becoming famous in the arts, such as sculptor Benno Schotz, artist Joseph Herman or the well-known writer Chaim Bermant – a few names from a much longer list of talented Glasgow Jews. Much of the information about Glasgow's early Jewish community comes from the writing of Abraham Levy, Glasgow's first Jewish solicitor and amateur historian.

Today, the Jews of Glasgow remember their origins with pride and affection. An exhibition in 1984 by the Gorbals Fair Society in the Adelphi Centre was as much a celebration of these origins as it was a mark of present-day Jewish identity and a testament to the 70-year history of the Jewish Representative Council in the city.

In 1965 the Board of Guardians set up a house purchase scheme for the Jews of the Gorbals, to help them move out and buy homes in the more attractive parts of the city. Jewish connections with that part of Glasgow, which had sheltered immigrants and refugees, and which had been the 'shtetl' of so many, were finally coming to an end.

The Glasgow Jewish community is now smaller than it was, yet most of its families still identify with the synagogues, the Jewish day school, which has existed since 1962, and the many Jewish welfare, youth, social and cultural organisations. None of this means, however, that the children or grandchildren of those immigrants who found a life in the city forego their common identity as Glasgow people, if the sentiments expressed by Ellis Sopher are typical:

'Glasgow 1970'

Yet even though I castigate this slattern Who has more right than

I to make a saturnalia of all her faults and misdemeanours too
Being born of her, Glaswegian through and through.

Kaplan and Hutt, *A Scottish Shtetl*

Jews have had a significant presence in Glasgow since at least the beginning
of the 19th century. The population now is believed to be between 5,000
and 6,000. The latest official record, the 2001 Census of Scotland, however, identified this group by religion only. Thus, it is recorded that 0.49
per cent of the population of Greater Glasgow was of the Jewish faith.
The 2011 Census, however puts the figure of 5,887 for all of Scotland.
(Scojec 2015) Today, the majority of Jews live on the South Side of the
city, mainly in the suburbs of Newton Mearns, Clarkston and Giffnock.
The community worships in five congregations – four Orthodox and one
Reform. The defining synagogue in the history of Jews in Glasgow, however, remains Garnethill. This Victorian listed building is home to the
senior congregation and the Scottish Jewish Archives.

The Archive Centre collects historical material relating to the Jews
of Scotland. Old synagogue minute books, thousands of photographs,
war medals and personal papers are all there to give a fascinating picture of Scotland's Jews. The centre is open to the public.

While there continues to be a range of social, educational and cultural
organisations serving the Jewish community in Glasgow, some aspects of
life have become more difficult, since, for example, there are no longer
any *kosher* butchers, and people rely on only two Jewish delicatessens
for their needs, or must obtain meat and other *kosher* products from
either Manchester or London.

Among the social and welfare organisations which have gone with
the passage of time are Glasgow Friends of Yiddish, the Jewish Choral
Society. The Glasgow Jewish Singers are still going strong. The community also benefits from table tennis club, an Israeli dancing group and a
preschoolers group.

In education, the long-established Calderwood Lodge is currently
embarking on an exciting new project. East Renfrewshire Council is
committed to building a new joint faith primary school campus for Jewish
and Catholic children, thought to be the first of its kind in Europe. The
existing Calderwood Lodge is to close its doors June 2017 when the primary and nursery school moves to the new campus in Newton Mearns.

Limmud Scotland, set up in 2001 continues to provide an innova-
tive learning and cultural environment for Jews. Moreover, the Scottish

Association of Jewish Teachers, now disbanded, is still available for consultation by the Scottish Government and the Scottish Qualifications Authority regarding Judaism in the Higher Religious Education curriculum.

There are, of course, also a range of welfare organisations that provide care for the city's Jewish community: Jewish Care Scotland, Cosgrove Care, the Glasgow Arklet Housing Association, the Jewish Blind Society, Newark Care **and Chai Cancer Care.**

Probably the most senior and brightest star in the firmament of Scottish Jews in the 21st century was Hannah Frank. The website relating to her life and achievements is simply headed 'Hannah Frank: A Glasgow Artist.'

Hannah Frank was born in 1908 in Glasgow, her father a refugee from persecution in Russia who settled in the Gorbals. He later opened a shop in Saltmarket for the sale of photographic and scientific equipment, which for 50 years was one of the best-known photographic centres in the city.

Hannah, one of four children, went to school in the South Side of the city, then studied at the University of Glasgow, graduating in 1930, having already published poetry and drawings in the university magazine. After teaching for a number of years in the East End, and attending classes at Glasgow School of Art, her talents were recognised in a series

Hannah Frank.

of prizes and exhibitions. Since the 1950s, Hannah concentrated on sculpture and her prolific and very personal style achieved international acclaim. Exhibitions of her work are frequently held in prestigious locations worldwide, and a documentary of her life was in production in 2007. August of this same year saw her reach 99 years of age, and the launch of a centenary year of celebration, crowned by an exhibition in Glasgow University in 2008 to coincide with her 100th birthday. Hannah lived in a care home in Glasgow, where a selection of her drawings and sculptures graced the surroundings for the edification of residents, staff and visitors. Hannah died in December 2008.

More than Hannah Frank, several successful products of the Glasgow Jewish community include J David Simons and prize-winning author and screen-writer David Solomons, the overall winner of Water-stone's Children's Book Prize in 2016. Another prize-win-ning author is Michael Mail, who won the prestigious Macallan Short Story Prize in 1999. He has since gone on to publish several novels that examine aspects of

The Garden.

Jewish identity. He also worked with UJIA an educational charity for the Jewish community.

Still flourishing is the Jewish Representative Council, the voice of the Jewish community in the west of Scotland since 1914, which celebrated its centenary in 2014 with many events. Under its president, Paul Morron MBE, 2013–2016 it conducted major reforms, and broadened its work to build political and religious ties with groups such as Glasgow City Council Muslim community. Recognised as a great orator, he has worked tirelessly for three turbulent years for the cause of religious tolerance.

The Jewish Representative Council also provides a democratic forum for synagogues and welfare, educational, social and cultural organisations, and disseminates news and information to and about the community.

Another main organ of dissemination is the Glasgow edition of the *Jewish Telegraph*, whose Scotland correspondent since 2006 has been Sharon Mail. It is the only regional Jewish newspaper in Britain. The local edition is a vital link to the Jewish world for the Glasgow community, maintaining a long-standing tradition begun with the *Jewish Echo* in 1928.

The umbrella organisation of the Jewish population is the Scottish Council of Jewish Communities (SCoJeC). Its purpose is to advance public understanding of Jewish religion, culture and community. SCoJeC works

The *Jewish Telegraph.*

in partnership with other organisations to promote good relations and equality, representing the Jewish community in Scotland to government and other statutory bodies, and liaises with members of the Scottish Parliament on issues affecting the community.

A disquieting matter that has been exercising both the Jewish community and governments alike is the rise of anti-Semitism across Europe in recent times. Of sufficient moment to warrant a government inquiry, a most basic comment, when the report was published, pointed out that:

> The inquiry was established to investigate the belief, widely held within the Jewish community, that levels of anti-semitism in Britain are rising. Following an investigation, we have reached the troubling conclusion that this belief is justified.
>
> *Report of the All-Party Parliamentary Inquiry into Anti-Semitism*, September 2006

Sadly, Glasgow has not entirely escaped this trend, with Garnethill Synagogue subjected to graffiti in August 2006, and a leading member of the Jewish community being the recipient of anti-Semitic mail.

On the other side of the coin, also in 2006, Kelvingrove Museum established a Holocaust section in the 'Conflict and Consequences' gallery of the newly refurbished museum. Within it, concentration camp survivors from the Jewish communities are honoured by means of their testimony and their art. And there has been the establishment of Gathering the Voices, project from 2014, which has collected testimonies from those who escaped the Nazis and made their home in Scotland. In collaboration with Glasgow Caledonian University GtV has developed a travelling exhibition which visits schools and other groups.

In 2014 SCoJeC, undertook a major inquiry into the lives of Jewish people in all parts of Scotland. The report *Being Jewish in Scotland* was presented to the Scottish Government in 2015. The inquiry was the product of a worrying increase in anti-Semitic incidents in Scotland in the latter part of 2014; a shock to the community both Jewish and otherwise. This comprehensive study of personal experiences and opinions revealed both the positive and negative aspects of being Jewish in Scotland at this time. Perhaps significant were the references to the rise of social media in incidents of anti-Semitism. (scojec.org.uk)

CHAPTER 5

The Glasgow Italians

BY THE LATE 20th century there were believed to be around 200,000 Italians in Britain, and in Glasgow alone there are few corners that have not known the tradition of Italian-owned cafés or fish-and-chip shops.

This tradition is changing, however, and although many Scottish Italians are still associated with the catering industry, in manufacturing, hotels or restaurants, there are just as many Scots–Italians to be found in all other walks of life. Some young people still arrive in Scotland from Italy, usually to work in the restaurant business for a while before returning to Italy, but most of the Italians in Glasgow are those who have been making the city their home for a very long time, their fathers or grandfathers among the Italian immigrants who came to Scotland as much as a century ago.

If we were to begin by looking at the very first Italians who came to Scotland, we would include those who were part of the Roman armies more than 2,000 years ago. For over four centuries the Romans controlled the part of Scotland where Glasgow was later to develop. Several centuries after the departure of the Romans, the next significant Italian presence in Britain was during the Middle Ages when Italian businessmen controlled the lucrative British wool trade. Italians led the world at this time in commerce and finance, and Italian bankers held the purse strings of more than one English monarch. At one point there was even a colony of Venetians in London who were powerful enough to mint their own currency.

Later, when Britain was better able to conduct her own commercial affairs overseas, the country became attractive to Italian merchants, artists and scholars and it became fashionable on the part of the aristocracy, Scottish as well as English, to dabble in aspects of Italian culture. Several Scottish monarchs were very much influenced by Italian culture and Italian musicians and artists were employed at the royal court. The most famous of these must be David Rizzio, counsellor and musician to Mary, Queen of Scots, who was murdered in the Queen's presence by a nobility jealous of his influence over her.

In the 18th century it became the done thing in polite society to speak

Italian as well as know about the music and art of Italy, and the 'Italian master' became a feature of the social life of these circles. But the people who were to become the foundation of the settled Italian community were of much more humble origin. In the 19th century they came in the wake of the poets and artists as itinerant street musicians and pedlars. Their presence in Glasgow is recorded by the same man who compared the Jews in Glasgow to 'Shylock' figures. He also saw the Italians as strange exotic creatures:

> The immigrants from Sunny Italy, who come to Glasgow and set up as music-mongers are also a noticeable feature in Sauchiehall Street's evening life. They trundle along their music machines, halt before some public house or restaurant, and grind out in the most business-like manner, 'Maggie Murphy's Home'... or some other ditty which happens to be enjoying its brief day of popularity... Queer people these swarthy Southerners of the lustrous eyes: the men with their seedy velveteen jackets and Bohemian neckties; the women, with their garish kerchiefs artistically twisted about their raven locks. The average Briton is inclined to rail against this foreign invasion but there are worse things than an organ manipulated by an Italian.
>
> Hammerton, *Sketches from Glasgow*, 1893

Many of the Italians who came to Britain were from the north of Italy, where there was a tradition of seasonal migration. People went abroad to work during the harsh Alpine winters and returned to their homes and their farming when good weather came again in the spring.

As the 19th century progressed, Italy experienced the same population increase as the rest of Europe, with the same effect on living standards as in the rural communities in Scotland and Ireland. In Italy, too, it meant that the land from which the majority of ordinary people scraped a meagre existence simply was not enough to feed all of this rising population. When people struggling with poverty heard of opportunities elsewhere, they were prepared to take the chance of finding something better, even if it meant leaving their homeland. Many Italians chose Britain but many more chose America. Even so, for some of those who came eventually to Scotland the road was quite hard enough. Dominic Crolla, a Glasgow Italian, discovered how hard:

I had a friend in Edinburgh whose father, when he died, we were all up in his house at night and we were looking for his birth certificate. When we came across it in a drawer we discovered that his father, in 1904 or 1905, had been born on the roadside between Dover and London. You see these people had walked from Italy, they'd got lifts on horses and carts and they made their way from the middle of Italy by road and track and boat to London.

Odyssey transcripts, BBC

Many of these people came to Britain under the influence of recruiting agents of the *padroni,* who were Italian patrons or employers. While the bulk of the *padroni*-related immigration to Britain centred on London, a number of people also made their way to Scotland. In Scotland, the *padrone* functioned as the employer and would often bring boys or young men from his own province, or even his own village, to work in the new country. Between 1890 and 1914 the Italian population of Scotland increased from about 750 to 4,500, a significant number of those in Glasgow itself. In 1891 a benefit society, the Societa di Mutuo Soccorso, was set up in Glasgow to lend money to Italians to start up in business.

Some of those who settled in Scotland had originally come from the *figurinai,* makers of statuettes, who came from a long tradition of itinerant craftsmen and pedlars. The *figurinai* are known to have originated from the Lucca area, and more precisely, from the town of Barga itself – the origin of a considerable proportion of the Glasgow Italian population of today. Terri Colpi tells the story of Leopoldo Guiliano, a *figurinai padrone,* who, after travelling with a group to the United States, reached Glasgow in the 1880s and decided to settle. By the turn of the century, Guiliano was the city's wealthiest Italian, owning no less than 60 cafés and shops.

In fact, Joe Pieri, author of *The Scots Italians,* writes that there were 336 ice cream shops and 4,000–5,000 Italians in Glasgow by 1905. Pieri also writes of the less savoury characters who emerged in the Italian community, notorious amongst them Serafini Rigordo, who set up a shebeen and house of ill-repute at Anderston Cross. Breaking the licensing laws by 24 hour trading Serafini was ultimately deported back to Italy for selling illegal alcohol. In his book Joe Pieri tells many colourful tales of the Italian immigrants, some favourable and others less so, like Serafini, but apparently it was not unusual for them to be cavalier with the local by-laws. One such was the Padrone, Mr Persichini, the owner of a cafe at the corner of Argyle Street and Union Street.In disregard for the law against Sunday opening Mr Persichini would have the police visit every week and be summoned to appear before the magistrate on Monday. Every week he did so and paid his £2 fine, just to return to his illegal ways the next Sunday. This went on until 1939, until he was arrested as an enemy alien and put out of business.

But Colpi also points out that it was the *ciociaria* from the province of Frosinone, whose origins lay in the joint traditions of street entertainment and street selling of food, who laid the foundations for the immigrant population to move into the catering business or as wig-makers, respectively, and it was from these traditions that the Italian connections with hairdressing are believed to have arisen.

Setting up in business for most Italians in Glasgow nevertheless meant getting into the ice-cream business, and later the fish-and-chip trade, and it has been suggested that it was the existence of the *padroni* that directed so many Italians into the ice-cream business. The making of ice-cream was an Italian speciality and was said to have been invented by the Romans. Regardless of who invented it, the Italians certainly exploited its potential as a source of business and 'ice-cream parlours', as the first cafés were called, appeared all over the country, many of them in Glasgow.

The Crolla family, some time ago, collecting ice from a factory in Laird Street in Bridgeton. Picture courtesy of Tania Sannino.

Many of the Italians who owned the ice-cream shops came from the same part of Italy, and in the late 1880s the majority of those who came to Scotland were from Lucca in the north and Frosinone, south of Rome. Groups of people from the same village would stick fairly closely together.

> When they came over all the people from their own village would come over and join them... so there's a big crowd from Barga – they've gathered together in Glasgow and the west.
>
> Odyssey transcripts, BBC

In those days, moreover, Italian parents were keen for their children to keep these links alive by marrying within the community; if they did marry Scots, it was preferred that they would be Roman Catholics, the religion of the vast majority of Italians.

All or most of this activity was prior to 1905 and the passing of the legislation known as the Aliens Order, which effectively reduced immigration from Italy. This legislation was not directly aimed at Italians, whose particular line of business hardly threatened the jobs of the native population, but was caused more by the alarm raised in the country by the mass arrival of refugees from Eastern Europe.

Not all Italians went into the food trade in Glasgow. In January 1908, an Italian language newspaper called *La Scozia* was first published in the city. It described itself as the 'paper for the Italian colony in Glasgow' and was published weekly at a cost of 4/4d (21.5p) for the year, or one penny for a single copy. The paper was owned by the Cafaro brothers, who also ran a library and bookstore in the city. It may well have been the Cafaro bookshop which sold Italian penny novelettes to homesick immigrants.

The publication of *La Scozia* also demonstrated that there were several other Italian businesses and organisations in Glasgow, including an Italian language school for adults and children in Union Street and the *Societa Dante Alighieri*, an institute for the preservation of the culture and language of the home country.

Besides those Italians who were in business in the city, there were also a number of immigrants who did the same kind of jobs as the native population, or suffered the same kind of hardship when they were unable to work. A survey into the diet of the labouring classes of the city, conducted between 1911 and 1912, looked at the living conditions of some Italian families among others. In one family, the father worked as a miner, in another the men of the family worked on the railways, but the study also looked at a family in which the father was unable to work because of ill health and depended on poor relief. This was their only source of income except 'when the mother gets a day's washing or goes out with an organ and a bird' – to become a street entertainer.

This family had 17 children, of whom only three young ones were still at home; the rest, presumably, were making their own way in the city. The survey suggested that all the working-class Italians studied found real Italian food from the Italian shops too expensive for them but they purchased and used a considerable amount of macaroni for traditional Italian cooking.

Most Italians were fairly well received in Glasgow. There were not as many of them as, for example, the Irish, and the service most of them provided in the food trade did not threaten the jobs of the native population in the way that the Irish were seen to do. There were some incidents, frequently the lot of people who are in the minority or are seen to be different in some way. One lady, who lived for many years in Glasgow, said this of her childhood in the city:

> When I used to go to school the kids used to pull my hair. I had jet black hair and they would tell me to speak Italian. I spoke

The Italian newspaper *La Scozia* has been carefully preserved in the Mitchell Library as a valuable record of one year in the life of the Glasgow Italian community: the last edition of the paper was published in December 1908.

Italian, I couldn't speak anything else. I couldn't even tell them to stop it.

Odyssey transcripts, BBC

Not everyone liked the kind of work the Italians did and the church in particular objected to ice-cream parlours opening on Sundays. The ice-cream shops were, in fact, open from 9 a.m. until 12 p.m. every day. Evidence given to a parliamentary committee on Sunday opening, which met in 1906, described the ice-cream shops as 'one of the evils of Glasgow'. The witness also said that young people who frequented these shops heard bad language and were encouraged to bad behaviour. The police also complained that there was much rowdiness in the ice-cream parlours and that they encouraged young people to 'hang about and loaf'. They also objected to the bad moral tone caused by billiard machines and automatic football games in the shops, and insisted that people were encouraged to gamble. It was even suggested that 'the Italian ice-cream man as a rule tolerates conduct in his shop that no Britisher would tolerate'.

Even in 1906, the prejudice in this accusation must have been self-

The Gizzi family business grew from its origins in the 1920s and '30s with a horse-drawn vehicle and then the Clyde Café, in Main Street, Bridgeton, to the Fulcreme factory in Stonelaw Road, Rutherglen.

Picture courtesy of Tania Sannino.

evident, since there was in Glasgow at this time a great deal of drunkenness, and much worse behaviour, than anything seen in the ice-cream shops. However, by 1913 Glasgow Corporation was reviewing the regulations regarding 'Places for Public Refreshment' and there were still attempts to close cafés and such places on Sundays (see page 91).

When the First World War came, Italian immigration to Britain was disrupted and, with the passing of the Aliens Act in 1919, which introduced work permits for foreigners, the numbers coming to this country stayed low. This meant that until after the Second World War, the number of Italians in Glasgow remained fairly static. In the city, the Italian community became quite settled, developing the food trade, while sons and daughters in some cases went into other jobs or professions. Although the café business was still predominant, in 1928 a college of Italian hairdressers opened in Glasgow, and many Italians are still associated with this kind of business.

The Fascist leader Mussolini seized power in Italy in 1923, and a branch of the Italian Fascist Movement was set up in Glasgow. By the outbreak of the Second World War, however, the existence of a Fascist organisation in Glasgow was unpopular, even though most Italians in the city claimed that it was regarded as little more than a social club. But when Mussolini joined Hitler and declared war on Britain on 10 May 1940, the Fascist Club and Italian businesses found themselves on the receiving end of violent attacks. The Italians had become the enemy and noisy anti-Italian demonstrations took place. The scale and intensity of the violence of that night left the immigrant community bewildered. It seemed as if the work of 50 or 60 years would vanish in the face of this hostility.

On 11 May 1940 the *Evening Citizen* reported the events of the previous night. A mob of 1,000 besieged a café on the Garscube Road, smashing the windows despite the presence of four policemen. Elsewhere, frightened Italians were escorted home to safety. Before the night was out, over 100 Italians had been detained as 'enemy aliens' and ice-cream and fish-and-chip shops throughout the city had been attacked. One ice-cream shop owner blamed Mussolini more than the people of Glasgow:

> I am Italian-born, but I have been a British subject for over 20 years... Although my shop has been smashed I am not going to go away. I am British. Only my name is Italian. I hope that when the people see me still here they will realise that, and let me live with them.

Worse was to come for the Italian community. *All* Italian men and women between the ages of 16 and 60 were to be arrested as 'enemy aliens' and sent to internment camps. Eventually, more than 1,400 Glasgow Italians were detained.

MORE ITALIANS HELD IN GLASGOW

The number of Italians being rounded up by the police in Glasgow is rising rapidly.

The total up to this morning was 350, but this will be raised by tonight to 500.

The Italians, both men and women, are between the ages of 16 and 60. Among them are about 100 naturalised and British-born subjects. They are being handed over to the military authorities.

To prevent a recurrence of the scenes after Italy had entered the war, extra constables patrolled the streets last night. Small crowds gathered at various points in the city, but they were dispersed.

Several shops owned by Italians not yet affected by the round up have remained open. The owners, British subjects, are displaying large notices in their windows stating 'We are British'.

Lord Provost Dollan, after a conference with Chief Constable Sillitoe, pointed out that the police had all the powers necessary to deal with Italians and other aliens. He said the attacks made on a few unprotected shops would involve the city in claims for damages and compensation.

The police had been instructed that hooliganism of the type masquerading as patriotism was to be stamped out.

'If people want to fight Mussolini,' Mr Dollan remarked, 'they can do so by joining the armed forces, working harder, saving more money, or joining one or other of the defence organisations.'

Evening Citizen, 12 June 1940

This is only one man's story, and there are many more, which shows what official policy meant to some of these ordinary people who had regarded Scotland as their home for many years:

That night... my wife she had a baby dying of pneumonia. Well the police came up to the house, it was about 11 o'clock. They says, 'You'll need to come with us.' I said, 'I don't know nothing about politics, I've been in Cambuslang most o' my days.' But anyway they took me to jail and of course I broke down because my wean was dyin'. The next day the wean died and the priest and doctor came and they asked the inspector if they would let me home for five minutes. He said 'No', so they took us away to the Isle of Man.

Odyssey transcripts, BBC

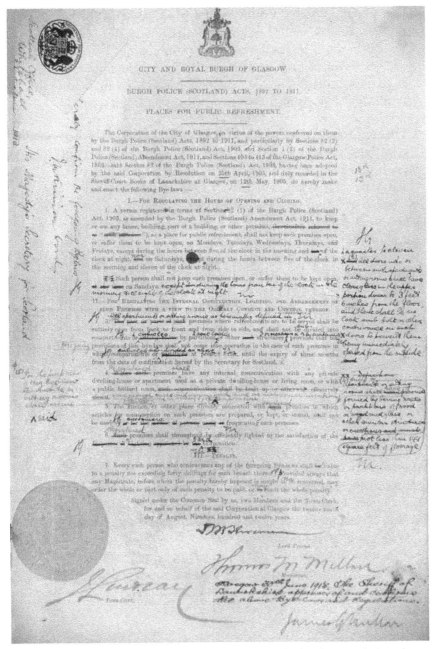

The many handwritten amendments on this document, the bye-law regulating places of public refreshment, show that the subject aroused considerable controversy in the Corporation in 1913.

Besides being interned on the Isle of Man, some of the 'aliens' were sent to Australia or Canada, and many Italians were lost going to Canada when their ship was torpedoed by a German submarine. Some of those who drowned were from Glasgow. The confusion that surrounded Glasgow's attitude to these Italians who had suddenly become 'enemies' after living in the city all their lives is clearly seen in this policeman's words:

I'll never forget the night Italy declared war and we locked up all the Italians... we had 10–12 Italians for about three days... there were a lot of decent Italians and there was a lot of sympathy for them: they were practically inhabitants of the place but they were all locked up... we knew some of them, had known them for years. They were enemies. Some of our lot were sunk on their way to Canada, they were torpedoed... When we went to the door some of them got a hell of a shock. They were as Glaswegian as we were, some were born in this country.

Odyssey transcripts, BBC

The almost incredible notion that these people were now dangerous aliens, who had to be locked up by people who had known them for years in some cases, is further emphasised by a story related by Colm Brogan in *The Glasgow Story* in 1952:

In June of 1940 a young Glasgow Italian was greatly distressed because his father had been put in prison as a first step towards internment. He had an interview with his father in prison and then closely questioned the broadly spoken typically Glaswegian sentry at the gate about possible anti-Italian prejudice. At first the sentry gave evasive and curt answers, and then, under persistent and detailed questioning, he became impatient and irritated. At last he could stand no more.
    'Ask me my name,' he said, in his richest Glasgow.
    'What's your name go to do with it?' the worried young man asked in natural surprise.
    'Ask me,' said the soldier stubbornly.
    'Well, what is it?'
    'Guidicci.'
    The worried young man was soon in the army himself...

In common with the sons of Jewish, Polish, or any other immigrants for that matter, most Italians accepted that their duty was to the country of their birth, even when their fathers were imprisoned by that country, which also happened to some of the German Jews in the city.

Most of the Glasgow Italians were home again by 1944 and within a few years the community was functioning again on normal lines. In 1951 more immigrants arrived under the 'Bulk Recruitment Scheme' agreed between the British and Italian ministries of labour. This scheme authorised immigration from Italy to fill labour shortages in agriculture, industry and coal mining. Those coming to work on farms had to guarantee four years' work on the farm and the women had to give a number of hours' compulsory work in hospitals.

Although about 150,000 Italians arrived in Britain under this scheme, not so many of them settled in Scotland, and some returned to Italy later. Those who stayed became part of a settled, close-knit community, which had gradually been eroded over the years by intermarriage and integration into the Scottish community.

A strong desire to keep the Italian identity alive in Glasgow, however, is shown by the continued existence of the Dante Alighieri Society, which maintains links between the members of the Italian community in the city and strengthens cultural links in language classes through lectures and visitors from Italy or other Italian communities. There is also the long-standing Scots Italian Golf Club, which still thrives from its founding in 1947.

Few of the young Italians who now come to Glasgow to work in pizza houses or restaurants settle here permanently but instead work for a few years and return to Italy. As for many Glasgow Italians of the third generation, however, it is suggested that while most of them appear to be completely assimilated into Scottish life in occupational or professional terms, closer inspection often reveals that an identifiable 'Italian' contact between people, businesses or professions is still detectable. A social and networking tool is available today in *Internations*, an online site for ex-pats, which has member events every month. And there are obviously still a number of Italians making the journey to the UK, and Scotland, to work mainly, since the Office of National Statistics records 59,000 Italian National Insurance registrations for year ending December 2015.

In these ways, Colpi suggests, an Italian presence is still 'distinguishable' in a Scottish context. If so, this must be welcome, since the same writer also points out that the traditional businesses of the Scottish

Italians – the cafés and 'chippies' – are now 'in a state of fossilisation and decline'. Those old-style cafés that still survive, and they are few in Glasgow, appear to the modern view as an anachronism: in Colpi's words, 'encapsulated in time'. But, for the record, these cafés serve another purpose, in that not only are they relics of a lifestyle that is passing, but remain, so far, a monument to the period that witnessed the evolution of the Glasgow Italian.

Tony Cimmino is joint owner, with his partner Claudio Nardoni, of the O Sole Mio restaurant. Established in the city centre in 1964, O Sole Mio is the oldest Italian restaurant in Glasgow.

Tony, who came to Glasgow from Rome in 1975 to work as a waiter, regards himself as 'wholly Glaswegian' and points out that this is the case for most Glasgow Italians now, who are fully integrated into the life of the city.

Besides which, any significant changes in the Italian presence in Glasgow today could not be recorded. Under the terms of the 2011 Census in Scotland, they would be classed as 'White Scottish' or 'Other White' by virtue of the Ethnic Identity question, which appeared in the 2001 Census for Scotland for the first time. Wikipedia, however, while not a wholly reliable source, stated that there are some 70,000–100,000 people of Italian descent in Scotland as a whole.

None of this, of course, is to suggest that an Italian presence in Glasgow is no longer evident. There remain many Italian restaurants and delicatessens, in addition to the Italian Centre in the Merchant City, a mecca for style and fashionable cafés. This particular project grew out of the ruins of derelict early 19th-century tenements; buildings that no doubt, in their day, were home to immigrants of many origins.

Most of the formal Italian institutions of Scotland today are based in Edinburgh – the Consulate General, the Italian Chamber of Commerce, the Ufficio Scolastico and the Centro Promozione Italiano. Glasgow, however, retains an honorary consul in Leandro Franchi, of Franchi Finnieston, solicitors and notaries in the city.

The late father of Leandro Franchi, Osvaldo, was a graduate in law of both the universities of Glasgow and Urbino in Italy. He was Italian Consul in Glasgow and a man of great commitment to the Italian–Scots community for many years.

Massimo Franchi, a managing partner of the law firm Franchi Finnieston, is also a sports agent. He represents a number of individuals in sport and is, in addition, an Official Licensed Players' Agent by the Scottish Football Association and FIFA, the governing body for world football.

Italian is spoken in the Franchi Finnieston law practice and the language is also taught in a number of classes in specialist language schools and at the universities.

There are a wide range of businesses in Glasgow run by people of Italian origin, but several also feature prominently in other spheres. Amongst those of Italian descent born in Glasgow is Sharleen Spiteri, who fronts the successful band Texas. Sharleen was born in 1967, the same year as Peter Capaldi, a well-known Scots actor and director. Linda Fabiani, member of the Scottish Parliament for the Scottish National Party, was born in Glasgow in 1956. And, perhaps most surprising in the history of Italian influence in Glasgow, is the entry in the online encyclopaedia Wikipedia for Elish Angiolini QC, who became Lord Advocate of Scotland in October 2006; a historic appointment, as the first woman to hold this post. Mrs Angiolini is listed as an Italian Scot, from the connection with her husband Dominico, a former hairdresser in Glasgow.

Finally, it is an interesting reflection on the rapidly changing ethnic and economic culture of Glasgow in the 21st century that Tony Cimmino, in the oldest Italian restaurant in the city, now employs both Polish and Nigerian staff.

CHAPTER 6

The Glasgow Polish Community

ANOTHER GROUP OF people who have made Glasgow their home, but whose origins lie elsewhere, is the Polish community of the city. Many of the Poles, or their descendants who live here now, came to Scotland during or after the Second World War, but Scottish links with Poland go back very much further than that.

As early as the 14th and 15th centuries, travelling merchants and Scottish mercenary soldiers made their way to Poland, and many settled there. During this period, a Scot named Andrew Chalmers was three-times Mayor of Warsaw, the Polish capital.

Later, in the turbulent 17th and 18th centuries, thousands of Scots emigrated to Poland as traders, artisans or soldiers, and records show that there were about 30,000 Scottish families living in Poland at the beginning of the 17th century. The troubles that beset Poland in the following century put an end to Scottish emigration to Poland and traffic began flowing in the opposite direction. Some Polish students came to Edinburgh University to study theology, but others were refugees from the 'battleground' that was Poland for generations. One historian, Norman Davies, has written, 'few people have doubted that Poland's geography is the villain of her history' (*History Today*, November 1982).

Set in the middle of the north European plain, Poland had no natural frontiers to ward off the territorial ambitions of much larger neighbours – Sweden, Austria, Russia, Germany and even France. Poland became a pawn in the power game played by these neighbours and from the first Russian 'protectorate' at the beginning of the 18th century onwards, the country became the scene of 'endless wars, risings, invasions, famines and epidemics'.

By the end of the 18th century, Poland had been partitioned between the other great powers more than once. In 1815, at the end of the Napoleonic Wars, when the Congress of Vienna met to rearrange the map of Europe, much Polish territory, including the capital city Warsaw, was awarded to Russia. In 1830, the Polish army rose against this foreign control. When the uprising was finally crushed in 1831, the Polish army was disbanded. Some of those involved who had to flee for their lives came to Scotland and settled in Edinburgh.

The first Scottish–Polish Society was founded in the 1830s by some of these refugees, to inform the Scottish people and to seek their support in publicising the plight of their oppressed countrymen in Poland. To this end, *The Polish Exile* was published for a time in Edinburgh and was also sold in Glasgow.

This small periodical, published throughout 1833, dealt with the history, politics and literature of Poland. Its purpose was to inform on the one hand, and to give moral and emotional support to Polish exiles on the other. The title, *The Polish Exile,* acknowledged the feeling, always evident among Poles resident in other lands, that they were exiled from their homeland by force of circumstances. Two verses from a poem published in the paper at this time clearly express this sense of separation and the ties that bind them to Poland.

A MEETING

OF THE

Society of Ladies,

IN AID OF THE INSTITUTION FOR EDUCATING THE YOUTH OF POLISH REFUGEES,

UNDER PRESIDENCY OF

PRINCE CZARTORYSKI,

Will take place on Tuesday, the 21st. of May, in the WATERLOO ROOMS, at One o'clock, P.M.

The Society hopes that the Inhabitants of this City will come forward to testify their sympathy for the unfortunate Poles, and to assist the object of this Institution.

Edinburgh, May 15, 1833.

The Polish Exile was produced by Polish refugees in Scotland in 1833 and this advertisement was a plea for support in setting up a school or college for educating the children of this exiled group.

'A Polish Exile's Address to his Country'

Alas! beloved Poland, the sword of the foe
Hath spread o'er thy plains desolation and woe;
It hath chased from their dwellings the brave and the free,
And thou has no longer a shelter for me.

My brothers they fly, or in battle they fall,
Or, they pine in their chains for they loved thee too well;
And I far must wander, an exile, from thee,
For thou hast no longer a shelter for me.

In 1863, another Polish rising against the Russians took place. This, too, was violently crushed and the very name of Poland was abolished. The troubles of the ravaged country were known far and wide. One of the songs published by the Poet's Box in Glasgow in 1868 shows, if the advertising is true, the interest in and popularity of the Polish cause in Glasgow.

FAIR LAND OF POLAND

PRICE ONE PENNY

Copies of this extremely popular song can only be had in the Poet's Box, 80 London Street, Glasgow

When the fair land of Poland
Was ploughed by the hoof
Of the ruthless invader; when might,
With steel to the bosom and flame to the roof,
Completed her triumph o'er right;
In that moment of danger,
When freedom invoked
All the fetterless sons of her pride,
In a phalanx as dauntless
As freedom e'er yoked,
I fought and I bled by her side.
My birth is noble, unstained my crest,
As is thy own – let this attest.

By 1914, the situation had not improved, and Poland was so divided that Poles found themselves fighting in the three armies of the partitioning powers – Russia, Germany and Austria. The Treaty of Versailles brought some regulation of the western borders, but the struggle continued to establish rightful possession of some eastern territories. The new Polish Republic set up by the Treaty of Versailles was a weakened state over-shadowed by powerful neighbours in east and west.

The Second Republic of Poland remained until Germany invaded the country on 1 September 1939 as part of Hitler's plan to control Eastern Europe while the new German Empire was established. Poland held out for one month, waiting for Britain and France to honour the terms of their agreement and attack Germany in retaliation. Hitler, in turn, had signed a non-aggression pact with Russia and he knew that there would be no threat from that direction when the Germans marched into Poland. Instead, Russia invaded Poland from the east on 17 September 1939. The Poles fought bravely but hopelessly, and once again it seemed that their country would be crushed out of existence between these powerful neighbours.

Those who could escaped to the west; first to France, where a Polish government-in-exile was formed, and then to London, when the Germans occupied France. For the vast majority of ordinary Polish people, however, escape was not possible and they had to suffer the full weight of Nazi oppression. Some were sent to Germany as forced labour, others were sent to Auschwitz and Majdanek:

> Most Poles can tell you how their brothers and friends were hanged or shot in the streets, how the womenfolk and children were transported in cattle wagons to the Reich or to Siberia, how they watched helplessly as the ss cleared their village or suburb of its peasants or Jews.
>
> *History Today*, November 1982

Many of the Polish people were Jewish and they were hunted down relentlessly – almost completely exterminated. When the Nazis crushed the Jewish uprising in the ghetto of Warsaw in 1943, they ended an association between the Jews and Poland which had begun in the 12th century. During the war, it is estimated that the Polish state lost six million of its citizens at the hands of the Germans, of whom more than five million were done to death as a matter of deliberate policy.

When the Polish government-in-exile was formed in London, under the leadership of General Sikorski, the First Army Corps, made up of some 40,000 Poles who had escaped, was set up with its base in Scotland.

King George VI and General Sikorski reviewing Polish troops in Lanarkshire
as the Polish forces join the fight against the common enemy.
Scottish Polish Society: *Historical Review.*

When the Polish soldiers came here, there were probably only a few thousand Polish-born people in Britain as a whole, apart from Polish Jews. From 1891 to 1911 – boom years for Scottish heavy industry – a significant number of the new arrivals in Glasgow alone were Polish or Russian: many were Jewish pedlars and tailors, but a considerable number were labourers and artisans drawn to these heavy industries or to the coal mines of the West of Scotland. Sometimes a miner would send home for a man to come and work alongside him, and the 1931 census shows several hundred Poles and Lithuanians working and living in Glasgow.

During the 1930s, as Nazi power spread across Europe, the numbers of refugees coming to Britain steadily increased. A refugee fund was set up in London in 1939 to assist those Poles who were being driven out or persecuted by the Nazis. Most were Polish Jews, and the *Jewish Echo* carried large notices on their behalf.

When Russia invaded Poland in 1939, some 1.5 million Poles were captured, but when the Nazi–Soviet pact collapsed in 1941 and Germany invaded Russia, the Soviet Union joined the Allies in the fight against Germany. A Polish army of deportees and prisoners of war was mobilised within Russia. This became the Polish Second Corps and was to see much military action before arriving in Britain in 1946. Eventually joined by their families – when they could be traced – these families became the backbone of the settled Polish community in Britain, and in Scotland in particular. Other elements joined the soldiers in Britain, among them some 21,000 prisoners of war liberated from German camps and brought to Britain by Polish units. Between 1945 and 1950 many of these people emigrated again, to America, Canada and Australia, and a few went back to Poland, but a considerable number stayed in Scotland, especially in and around Glasgow. Typical of many who made Scotland their home is Mr Wladyslaw Bednarek, Chairman of the Polish Social and Educational Society until 1991.

As a young man, Wladyslaw Bednarek lived in a rural community in Eastern Poland. At the beginning of 1940, Mr Bednarek, his wife, two brothers and his sister were among the 1.5 million arrested. They were taken to the Archangel District in the Soviet Union and put to work cutting timber. When Russia joined the allies and an amnesty from slave labour was granted in 1942, Mr Bednarek and his brother became part of the Polish Second Corps. While his mother and sister were sent as refugees to camps in East Africa, Wladislaw found himself on active service in France and Austria and was part of the army of occupation until 1947, when, with other parts of the Polish army, he came to Scotland. The Bednarek family has lived in Glasgow since 1949, Mr Bednarek eventually becoming a partner in a wholesale delicatessen business. While his son and daughter were born in Scotland, they still retain their links with the Polish homeland, as do many other Polish people in the area.

When Mr Bednarek and his family came to Scotland they became part of a group of about 8,000 Polish people who were in Scotland during and after the war. A number of organisations had been set up to serve this Polish community, particularly in Glasgow. The Scottish Polish Society, inaugurated in December 1941, was a national organisation in that there were active branches in many parts of Scotland, and the Glasgow branch was very strong. Much of the Society's aim was to foster relations between the two countries when the war would be over, and to raise funds for the soldiers and provide social and cultural connections between the existing Polish and Scottish communities. Sir Patrick Dollan, himself of Irish immigrant origin, and a prominent Glasgow politician, was an energetic supporter and office bearer of the Society for several years.

10, Downing Street,
Whitehall.

On behalf of the Government and people
of Great Britain, I am very glad to write
this line of welcome to every Polish soldier,
sailor or airman who has found his way over
to help us fight and win the war.

I have heard of the difficulties which
have beset your journeys to this country: I
realise the hardships which your relatives
and friends are undergoing in Poland: but I
know that these will only inspire you to
further deeds of endurance and valour for
which your nation is so justly renowned.

Until the hour comes when through our
united efforts you return to your own country,
we in Great Britain hope that you will find
amongst us a happy, if temporary, home.
Together with our joint Allies, we look forward
to the day when victory will crown our efforts
and we shall help to build a new and better
Europe.   I know that the Polish forces on
land and sea and in the air will play a worthy
part in achieving this goal.

Winston S. Churchill

3rd September, 1940.

The letter sent by Winston Churchill to welcome Polish troops to Britain.
Scottish Polish Society: *Historical Review.*

Also in 1941, an organisation called 'The Polish Hearth' was opened, as a centre for Polish civilian refugees and servicemen, and the facilities of the centre included a dispensary where free medical treatment was available to these people. Dr Jan Aigen, himself a refugee from Warsaw, where he had continued to work for almost a year after the Nazi occupation, was in charge of the dispensary. Later, Dr Aigen was to describe his experience in a book called, simply, *I Saw Poland Suffer*.

In September 1942, the Polish President came to Glasgow to open a school for Polish students at Dalbeth in the East End of the city.

Polish President in Glasgow

At the new school which has almost 200 students – some of them elected by their units in the services while others are refugees who escaped from Poland through Russia... a preparatory course will qualify successful candidates for admission to Polish universities after the war.

The President, who congratulated the students on their excellent physical appearance and cheerfulness, said that young Poland was preparing for the regeneration of a country that could never be conquered...

At an informal reception for officials of the Scottish Polish Society... Sir Patrick Dollan, proposing the toast of Poland, said that Scotland was proud to be associated with a country which had a firm friendship with Caledonia 500 years ago and had maintained it throughout many vicissitudes.

Glasgow Herald, September 1942

In 1943 the Polish Commercial College was opened in Cowcaddens Street. The college director, Professor Dombrovsky, later became a lecturer in Polish at Glasgow University. The college specialised in commercial subjects but also taught Scottish Highers and Lowers and Cambridge certificate work, as well as Polish language and culture.

These organisations, as described by the Polish President, were intended to prepare the Polish people – civilian refugees and soldiers alike – to return to their homeland to pick up anew the threads of Polish national life. However, for many Poles this was not to be. When the war ended and territories in Eastern Europe were absorbed into the Soviet Union, and when a Communist government was set up in Poland, several thousand Poles chose to stay in Scotland.

Most of them – about 80 per cent in fact – were Roman Catholics and as such mixed with and married into the Roman Catholic community of Scotland. The Poles also supported each other, however, and continued to do so after the war when many thousands of displaced Poles, whose homes, families and livelihoods had been shattered by the war, were settled in Britain under the Polish Re-Settlement Act. Thousands more were attracted to Britain by the recruitment schemes devised by this country to bring in Poles and other Eastern Europeans to fill the labour shortages created by the war. Between 1946 and the 1950s Britain experienced immigration from Eastern Europe on a far greater scale than that which came from the New Commonwealth countries in the 1960s. More than 300,000 Europeans migrated to the United Kingdom and added to the many thousands of Poles and other Eastern European refugees who had been in Britain since the war.

After the war, therefore, organisations were still being founded in Glasgow to help serve the needs of the Polish community. The Polish Ex-Combatants Association is still in its original premises in the West End of the city, and close by is the Polish Social and Educational Society, which opened in 1954. More commonly known as the 'Polish Club', the society now has about 400 members, consisting of both first- and second-generation Poles. The club, is where Poles and Scottish Poles, and interested Scots for that matter, meet to be reminded of, or to learn about, the culture, language and traditions of the land of their forefathers. Between 30 and 40 children attend the Polish language classes held there on Saturdays.

This plaque can be seen on the wall outside Sikorski House, the headquarters of the Polish Social and Educational Society.

The Polish people of Glasgow still have strong cultural and emotional ties with Poland and few scenes could have been more emotional for Scottish Poles than the dedication of the Katyn memorial in Glasgow in April 1984. In April 1943 reports emerged from a little place called Katyn, in Russian territory close to Smolensk, that a mass grave had been found. A ditch, some 28 metres long and 12 metres wide, was discovered, in which lay the bodies of 3,000 Polish army officers. They were described as

> fully dressed, in military uniforms, some were bound, and all had pistol shot wounds in the back of their heads.
>
> *The Crime of Katyn*

Other mass graves of executed prisoners of war were found, and this horrific event has become known in history as the 'Crime of Katyn'. In memory of this atrocity, the Glasgow Polish community held a mass in St Simon's Church on 29 April 1984, and a plaque dedicated to the victims of Katyn was unveiled by the Lord Provost of Glasgow, Michael Kelly. In 1990, the Russian government finally accepted responsibility for this massacre, and offered an apology to the people of Poland.

Poles in Glasgow today keep in touch with events in Poland and news of the British Polish community by means of the Polish language newspaper, the *Dziennik Polski* (Polish Daily), which is published in London.

In a historical review of the Scottish–Polish Society and its activities during and after the war, Dr Leon Koczy told the story of some these immigrants, who, in his words, 'although Polish by heart... are entirely loyal to their adopted country'.

In the 1990s there were about 3,000 Polish-born residents in Scotland, but their children and grandchildren identify with their Polish origins and are proud of their dual cultural heritage while they take full part in the life of Scotland – working in trades or businesses, the professions or the universities. In 1980, Dr Koczy concluded his publication with the reasons for the affection the Polish people have for their adopted land:

> The romanticism and high excitement of wartime faded away long ago. But there is something which will remain in the history and traditions of both nations – Scottish and Polish. This is the fact that at one time the Polish soldiers side by side with their Scottish comrades fought and died for a common cause and that when lonely and far from their families they found in Scotland hospitality, friendship, understanding and goodwill.

Polish Community welcomes the Pope

Polish Catholics have a special interest in the visit of His Holiness Pope John Paul II. Andrew Collier has been investigating.

Poles living in Scotland cannot, by and large, look back on a happy history. Most of their lives here have been tinged with a sad irony: they originally came to Britain under the shadow of war to defend a freedom denied to their native land by Hitler.

The tragedy is that their beloved Poland, more than 40 years on, has not seen liberty yet.

MAY 1982 1

The present-day Polish community in Glasgow shared in Poland's pride as the birthplace of John Paul II, the first Polish Pope in the history of Christianity, when Pope John Paul II came to Glasgow in 1982. *Scottish Field*, May 1982.

Migrant Workers in Glasgow Today

Polish bus drivers, Czech care workers and Latvian bricklayers are just a few of the many examples of Glasgow's migrant workers. Encouraged by the changing dimensions of the European Union and a relatively healthy labour market, thousands of citizens from the new Member States of the European Union (EU) have migrated to Britain.

However, immigration law in the United Kingdom is complicated: Commonwealth citizens, European Union citizens, people from the European Economic Association and foreign nationals must all meet quite different criteria in order to reside and/or work in this country.

At the beginning of November 2006, reports indicated that immigrants were arriving in the United Kingdom at the rate of 1,500 people a day, and it was claimed that at least 600,000 people had come to this country since the enlargement of the EU to 25 Member States in 2004.

The new migrants have come mainly from the Central and Eastern European states of the Czech Republic, Estonia, Latvia, Lithuania, Slovenia, Slovakia, Hungary and Poland. These have become known as the Accession 8 (A8) states, although Malta and Cyprus have also entered the EU. While free movement of people is a fundamental principle of EU membership, a temporary deviation from this commitment was permitted to help Member States ensure a smooth adjustment to enlargement. In 2004, however, the United Kingdom, together with two other states, decided not to make full use of a transitional period of seven years, during which they could apply some limitations on the entry of people from the A8 countries. While only Sweden opened the door fully to migrants from the new states, the United Kingdom and Ireland welcomed those able to find work, but restricted access to unemployment benefits to prevent attracting 'benefit tourists'.

The European Commission is keen to see all Member States be more open to the A8 migrants, but most of the existing countries, such as France and Germany, have remained cautious about unrestricted access. This situation somewhat diluted the effect of 2006 as 'The European Year of Workers' Mobility'. In any case, as yet, only two per cent of EU citizens live in a country other than that in which they were born.

However, such large-scale movement of workers from east to west is not without its critics. There is concern that better wages and working conditions in the west are likely to drain young talent from poorer countries, which will then be denied the opportunity to prosper economically. The fact that many of these workers felt the need to migrate is well under-stood, since most of the new EU states have serious unemployment prob-lems: in Poland, for example, unemployment stands at 20 per cent. Further motivation to leave includes much lower earnings and inferior working conditions in the accession states.

The UK Government and most employers' organisations argue that the influx of workers since 2004 is beneficial to this country:

> Immigration into the UK from new member states has been a success story... benefiting the economy, business and the people who have come. Employers rate migrants highly on effort, commitment and willingness to work.
>
> Confederation of British Industry, 2006

From the late 1980s and the break-up of the former Eastern Bloc, the United Kingdom welcomed a steady trickle of migrants, but by 2006 that trickle had become a powerful flow – 82 per cent between the ages of 18 and 34. However, all A8 migrants coming to the United Kingdom to work are expected to register with the Home Office if they plan to work for more than a month. The Workers' Registration Scheme requires migrant workers to complete and send documentation to the Home Office, together with a fee of £70.

The Government's case for registration is that it is necessary to log migrant workers into the tax system. The scheme has been much criticised, however, for failing to establish a penalty for non-compliance, thus encouraging illegal working.

In Scotland, the Federation of Small Businesses spoke for many companies relying on migrant labour with their claim that the fee created a block on workers from poorer states, because for some, £70 could amount to more than one month's wages in their home country. This particular scheme was closed on 30 April 2011 for migrants from the new accession countries.

In the United Kingdom most of the new workers have come from Poland – the most recent figures showing that 61 per cent of migrants are Polish, 12 per cent are Lithuanian and some 10 per cent Slovakian. A similar breakdown is found in the Scottish context.

In August 2006, the Home Office reported that some 32,000 Poles had settled in Scotland. These figures, however, show only those who have registered for work, and do not include self-employed workers. They are further complicated by the fact that the Home Office keeps no register of A8 migrants leaving the country, either to return to their home countries or, for that matter, to other EU states.

In Glasgow, anecdotal evidence puts the number of Poles at around 20,000, a figure which, as explained above, is fluid. Nevertheless, it would seem to be the case that the Polish influx to Scotland in general was encouraged by the then Scottish Government minister Tom McCabe, when he made a visit to Poland to launch a welcome pack for migrant workers. To date, most of these workers have been absorbed into the hotel and catering trades, while some have found employment in offices, agriculture, food-processing and manufacturing industries.

For the most part, migrant workers have been welcomed in Glasgow and are seen to boost Scotland's declining population and skills shortages. Glasgow City Council in particular has made considerable effort in this: their website gives details of its own 'Welcome to Glasgow' information pack for migrant workers, which has been published in Polish and Slovakian and can be downloaded in these languages from the site. This comprehensive pack provides information on the following: finding work; rights at work; finding accommodation; living in the community; safety (fire, police, crime, driving); health; and the right to stay in the United Kingdom.

In addition to such initiatives, Poles who come to Glasgow are in the fortunate position of being able to access the long-standing Sikorski Polish Club.

The Sikorski Polish Club, or the Polish Social and Educational Society, has been in the West End of Glasgow since 1954. Prior to 2004 and the new migrants, there were thought to be about 1,000 Poles, or people of Polish descent, in the city. Today, time-honoured Polish institutions in Glasgow, such as the clubs and the church of St Simon, help provide a secure infrastructure

Glasgow City Council's 'Welcome Pack' for migrant workers.

for the new arrivals. The church, which bears a plaque commemorating the Polish soldiers who came to hear mass in their native tongue during the Second World War, continues to have a service in Polish each Sunday.

The Sikorski Club is a focal point and invaluable source of activities and information for Poles in Glasgow. Open six days a week, the club is also a centre for rest, recreation and education. There is a restaurant serving Polish food, and a mother and toddler group, games room, library, bar and Polish television broadcasts. It also provides free English language classes, as do several other organisations, such as Glasgow University and the Annexe Healthy Living Centre in Partick. The club boasts a five-a-side football team, which has benefited from the presence of so many young Poles in Glasgow. In June 2006, the team, for the third year running, took part in the 'Show Racism the Red Card' football tournament. Live coverage of European international matches involving Poland are shown at the club, sponsored by the Western Union Money Transfer Company. And in November 2006, Poles in Glasgow also had an opportunity to dine at Parkhead stadium with Celtic Football Club's Polish stars.

Another home-grown talented Pole is Adrian Wiszniewski. Born in Glasgow in 1958, he studied at Glasgow School of Art before going on to win many distinctions in the art world, exhibiting at home and abroad and enjoying a stellar career in 2016.

In 2016 the club is as lively as ever, as their website confirms, and is currently restoring and renewing the fabric of the original building in Parkgrove Terrace, with a dedication ceremony planned for late 2016. Anna Maria Anderes, daughter of the famour General Anders, intends to be there, as do several other dignitaries from Poland and Scotland.

The society is also now a Registered Scottish Charitable Incorporated Organisation.

Hey Now, a Polish–British magazine founded in 2003, also attests to the Polish presence in Glasgow. Targeting Polish immigrants, *Hey Now* is devoted to historical and cultural matters, and current affairs. The magazine extended to Scotland, as does Radio Hey Now, an Internet radio station. Broadcasts are mainly in Polish, with some English, and every Sunday the programme 'Glasgow Voice' featuring Andrew Elliott of the Sikorski Club.

While the situation appears to be relatively healthy for the Polish community in Glasgow, some migrants do face very real problems. On 6 October 2007 the Global Migrants' Day demonstration in Glasgow raised some concerns. The Transport and General Workers' Union invited Polish workers and their families to a meeting, also in October, to discuss issues regarding living and working in Glasgow. Amid concerns about the abuse of migrant workers' rights, the Union and the Catholic Church joined forces to help these workers, particularly those from Poland. The Archbishop of Glasgow, Mario Conti, said:

I am delighted to work with the Union and offer support and solidarity to newly-arrive Poles and their families'.

Daily Record, 16 September 2006

Concerns over the problems encountered by migrants were also expressed by Citizens Advice Scotland, who reported that increasing numbers of migrant workers were approaching them to complain of low pay, long hours and sub-standard accommodation. These problems were compounded by language difficulties and a lack of understanding of basic workers' rights. Citizens Advice Bureaux across the country were hearing of exploitative employers, and employment agencies paying below the national minimum wage and making illegal deductions. Further difficulties were encountered regarding statutory sick pay, holiday entitlements and tax documents such as P45s and P60s.

Some migrants also told of living in overcrowded caravans, being expected to share sleeping arrangements and being overcharged for rent and utilities. Since all of this is organised by the employment agencies, some feared that complaints may have led to dismissal and homelessness. Kaliani Lyle, Chief Executive of Citizens Advice Scotland, said:

Workers have told bureaux of being given false expectations or wrong information about their employment prospects while still in their countries of origin. Once in the UK, however, their options are few.

Citizens Advice Scotland, press release, June 2006

Migrants were also experiencing problems in opening bank accounts and were often forced to use expensive cheque-cashing services to cash their wages. National Insurance numbers and work permits also presented difficulties for some, while those who needed to access the benefits system might have been left destitute. Citizens Advice Scotland saw a need to produce information in a range of languages, which could be made available to migrant workers on arrival in the United Kingdom or before they have left their home countries.

Moreover, the Sikorski Club website warned of a rather sinister problem in November 2006. In some cases, migrants were being met at airports or stations by individuals posing as employment agents who, for a sum of money, made false promises of work and accommodation, before disappearing and leaving their victims destitute and homeless.

In Glasgow, the Polish Taste delicatessen in the West End has become something of a gathering place for young Poles in the city. The deli is run by the Korzeniowski family, and their son Bartek, who is a student at Glasgow University. Bartek told the *Sunday Herald* in August 2006 of how many young Poles regard immigration:

> Is Britain my home? No. The point about immigration is that it is very fluid. It is not difficult to get a flight tomorrow and go somewhere else to start your life.

Younger migrants see themselves as European citizens and relish the freedom to move around the EU. Bartek's parents' motivation for coming to Glasgow was simply the desire for a life change. However, most migrants are looking for better jobs and the chance to make some money.

Unlike more visible immigrants, Poles tend to be spared the extremes of British racism, and Bartek voiced the opinion of his contemporaries when he pointed out that: 'all in all, Scottish people are very friendly' (*Sunday Herald*, 27 August 2006).

Another Pole who has lived in Glasgow for a considerable time is Professor Anna Dominiczak. In October 2006 she was named Scotswoman of the Year (*Evening Times*, October 2006). Originally from Gdansk, she has spent almost 30 years in the city working on researching heart disease and helping to secure funding for a major new international centre dedicated to reducing heart disease.

Since 2004, however, Professor Dominiczak, in common with all the migrants from the A8 states to Scotland, has had the right to vote in the Scottish Parliament and local council elections. The Scottish National Party (SNP) in particular has been quick to spot a potential source of new votes.

The SNP – or *Szkocka Partia Narodowa* – was anxious to capture the votes of the 50,000 Polish immigrants who were believed to have arrived in Scotland. To this end, in October 2006 the party sent out registration cards in Polish underlining the fact that A8 migrants had the right to vote in the 2007 Holyrood elections. Party chiefs saw Poland's own

Polish Taste, a Polish delicatessan.

history of independence from the former USSR may be an incentive. Peter Murrell, SNP Chief Executive, explained:

> They [the Poles] are benefiting from independence from the Soviet State and are therefore more open to the message that Scotland is an ancient, independent country
>
> *Scotland on Sunday*, 29 October 2006

The SNP targeted those seats where there was a large concentration of Polish people – such as Glasgow Govan and Glasgow Kelvin. Marcin Klessa, then manager of the Sikorski Polish Club, said he had received Polish literature from the SNP: 'I like the idea to see Scotland become a sovereign nation.'

Politicians, however, were not alone in grasping the opportunities presented by thousands of Poles in Scotland. While the official Home Office figure of 32,000 at September 2006 accounted for those who had registered for work, it was thought that when students, the self-employed and families entered the equation the figure may be closer to 50,000. Thus, Lloyd's TSB Scotland was printing banking literature in Polish and hired Polish speakers at certain branches. Employers advertise on Polish language websites and the Scottish Government has set up its own Polish language website for new arrivals.

The Scotsman online news site, however, reported in October 2006 that local council staff in certain areas felt that they were being swamped by requests for assistance from migrants, to the detriment of their services to the indigenous population. Politicians, on the other hand, were more inclined to see these difficulties as the initial effects of unprecedented numbers of migrants coming to Scotland, which would sort out themselves in time. The government's position on these figures is that they are an indication of the success of the Fresh Talent initiative in Scotland: 'It shows Scotland is a contender to attract bright, hard-working people' (*Daily Record*, 25 August 2006).

The Fresh Talent initiative as such was designed specifically to encourage graduates to work in Scotland. Working with the Home Office, the scheme was launched in 2005. Together with a one-step service, the Relocation Advisory Service (RAS), thousands of inquiries were generated from prospective students in more than 140 countries around the world in the first year, while a website on living in Scotland was accessed by half a million visitors by the latter part of 2006.

Conditions for entry to Scotland under the Fresh Talent scheme require that anyone from a non-European Economic Association country graduating from a Scottish higher or further education institution with an HND, first degree, masters degree or PhD is eligible to apply for leave to remain in Scotland for a further two years, without applying for a work permit. International students, in fact, have been recognised as a key audience for the Fresh Talent initiative, and a number of measures have been put in place to support them: these include the Scottish International Scholarship Programme, the 'Fresh Talent: Working in Scotland' scheme, together with the Supporting International Students Challenge Fund. This fund has been set up to help universities and colleges provide students with

> opportunities to enjoy all that their new home has to offer and make decisions about whether to stay in Scotland at the end of their studies
>
> Scotlandistheplace.com

Yet another route into Scotland is provided by the UK-wide Highly Skilled Migrants Programme. This programme is designed to allow highly skilled people to migrate to the United Kingdom to look for work or self-employment opportunities. It is a points-based immigration scheme, scored against five criteria: educational qualifications; work experience; past earnings; achievements in chosen field; and spouse, partner's or civil partner's achievements. The scheme ended in 2008.

It is an inescapable fact of life, nevertheless, that where there are genuine opportunities for the many, there will be a few unscrupulous opportunists who find ways to undermine them, such as the bogus employment agents who cheat new migrants with false promises, or the 'conmen' of Nigeria.

Eddie Barnes, political editor of *Scotland on Sunday*, reported on 1 October 2006 of the discovery made by his newspaper that fraudsters had hijacked the Scottish Government's flagship policy. The report went on to disclose the fact that the government's Fresh Talent initiative lay at the heart of this fraud. African students, approached by fraudsters posing as British airline officials, have been persuaded to part with large sums of money in return for clearance to come to Scotland under the Fresh Talent scheme. Officials in Nigeria, informed of the scam by the British High Commission, noted that they were aware of dozens of false schemes that exploit the thousands of Nigerians who, every year, attempt to emigrate to Britain.

On 1 January 2007, Bulgaria and Romania entered the EU as new Accession States, known as A2. In preparation for this, the Home Office made an announcement in October 2006. In the light of previous experience, it would appear, the United Kingdom decided to limit access to its labour market, although from 1 January citizens of these states have the right to travel throughout the EU. The ministerial statement from the UK government was as follows:

> Skilled Romanian and Bulgarian workers with the right qualifications and experience will continue to be allowed to come to the UK to take up specific jobs where no suitable UK applicant can be found.
>
> Romanian and Bulgarian workers with particularly high levels of skills and experience will continue to be admitted as they are now on the Highly Skilled Migrants Programme (pre 2008).
>
> Low-skilled migration from Bulgaria and Romania will be restricted to those sectors of the economy where the UK already low-skilled schemes and will be subjected to a strict quota which will not exceed 20,000 workers per year. The Workers Registration Scheme will continue to apply to nationals of the A8. WRS will not apply to Bulgarian and Romanian nationals.

In the same announcement, the Home Office minister explained the restrictions thus:

> We have decided to take a gradual approach this time round, taking account of the needs of our labour market, the impact of and the positions adopted by other member states... Through this measured response to accession we will ensure that migration is, and continues to be, managed in the best interests of the country as a whole.
>
> Written ministerial statement, 24 October 2006

Another element in the migration picture, of course, is the fact that recent reports place the number of British people migrating from the United Kingdom to be in the region of 1,000 a day. This, no doubt, has a proportionate effect on the population of Glasgow.

CHAPTER 7

The Chinese in Glasgow

IN 1953 THERE were only three Chinese families living in Glasgow; in the 1990s, there were believed to be about 3,000 Chinese people living and working in the city. To refer to the 'Chinese community' is to speak of people from the Republic of China, Taiwan and Hong Kong – and other parts of South-East Asia, such as Malaysia (where there was, for a long time, a large Chinese population), but the majority of the Chinese people who live in this country came originally from Hong Kong, which was a Crown Colony of Britain from 1842 to 1997. In 1914, the Imperial Act determined that 'everyone born within the allegiance of the Crown in any part of the Empire' was a British subject: as such, they had the right to move to other parts of the Empire if they so wished. People from Hong Kong have therefore emigrated to Britain at various times during the previous century, but mostly during the 1950s and 1960s.

Around 1800, Britain did not have a very strong foothold in the Far East, but British merchants, always working to expand their interests through the capture of foreign markets, were increasing trade with China. In Britain there was an insatiable demand for one of China's main products, tea, which was imported in vast quantities in return for British goods. The British also sold the Chinese opium, an addictive drug, grown and exported from India to China. The British East India Company, authorised by the British government to control much of India's trade, extended British interest to China. For a number of reasons, the East India Company's monopoly on trade with China was terminated in 1833 and the British government itself became involved in direct dealings with the Chinese authorities. Historians agree that the British, always confident that, in any case, they could win the argument with the use of force, were brash and insensitive in their dealings with the Chinese. As opium imports increased and the Chinese authorities became worried about the effect the drug was having, both morally and economically, the Chinese government took steps to suppress the opium trade. But British merchants, seeing their profits endangered, put pressure on the British government to threaten the Chinese with force. Gradually, the disagreement developed into conflict.

The Governor General of Hapei and Hunan wrote to Queen Victoria:

> the barbarian merchants of your country, if they wish to do business for a prolonged period, are required to obey our statutes respectfully and to cut off permanently the source of opium... After receiving this dispatch will you immediately give us a prompt reply regarding the details and circumstances of your cutting off the opium traffic?

The British government's representative in Canton replied by ordering attacks on the Chinese. 'The Opium War', as it was known, began formally in June 1840. The British forces, particularly the Navy, were superior in technology and, reaching Hong Kong in 1841, forced the Chinese government into concessions. The concessions were mainly trading privileges in various ports but among them was the right to take control of the territory of Hong Kong. By the Treaty of Nanking in 1842, Hong Kong became a British Crown Colony. In 1860, after further conflict, the Chinese government ceded the Kowloon peninsula to Britain. The last accession of Chinese territory by Britain came from the pressure of other imperialist ambitions, such as those of France and Germany. British help in keeping them at bay was rewarded by another treaty, which extended the area of Hong Kong and gave a 99-year lease of further territory for the defence of the colony. This area became known as 'The New Territories', and the 99-year lease on these lands ended in 1997. Since the mid-19th century, however, the Chinese have established a tradition of emigration, and Chinese labour was to play a crucial role in late 19th-century economic developments of the British Empire. The Chinese also emigrated to South-East Asia and, in significant numbers, to America. In the modern Western world there are few major cities that do not have their own Chinese communities.

The earliest Chinese immigrants to Britain were sailors who lived in the dock areas of Liverpool and London. There are references to Chinese being in London as early as 1814. The few Chinese who stayed in Britain were seamen who, usually recruited from the New Territories' villages to serve aboard freighters, jumped ship in British ports.

One of these Chinese seamen who left his ship in Glasgow was the father of Jimmy Yee, who, between the wars, opened a small Chinese restaurant on Govan Road beside the docks. This was a modest restaurant, as were most of the others in Britain at this time. The Chinese also specialised in the laundry business, although there was to be much less need for this service when the washing machine arrived on the market in the 1950s. It was, therefore, the catering business that was to be expanded by the Chinese.

In the 1950s and 1960s Britain experienced a period of reasonable prosperity, with no shortage of work. People had more money in their pockets as a result and were developing a taste for foods that were a little out of the ordinary, including Chinese cuisine. Between 1956 and 1965 the Chinese restaurant trade in Britain grew rapidly – usually staffed by immigrants from Hong Kong.

In the early days of this immigration the great majority who came were men who would send for their families once they were settled in work and had somewhere to live. By the late 1960s, however, it had become more common for whole families to emigrate. There were, at this time, a number of reasons why many Hong Kong Chinese chose to come to Britain.

In 1978 the story of a Chinese family in Glasgow – the Lee family – was published in a book for schools called *The Phoenix Bird Takeaway*, the name of Mr Lee's restaurant on the South Side of the city. Mr Lee's family comes from Hong Kong, and he himself grew up in a small rural village called Sham Chung. Mr Lee's children, however, have grown up in Glasgow, and the little boy seen here in the Phoenix Bird kitchen is now a young man.

When the Communist Revolution took place in China in 1947, many people crossed over into Hong Kong, packing into the already crowded cities of Victoria or Kowloon and encouraging many of those with British passports to come to Britain to find work. The information from Chinese already in Britain, that the restaurant trade needed more labour, was soon passed back to many of the villages of the New Territories, and the young men, and then the families, would come to join the others already there. When whole families came very often the best way to get started was by opening a carry-out restaurant. This required less capital to start than a full restaurant.

The occasion marked by the picture on page 121 was the publication of a House of Commons Report on the Chinese in Britain in January 1985. Concern was expressed then about the fact that many Chinese people in this country were excluded from the range of benefits in the society to which they were entitled as British citizens. The report concluded that this was partly due to the traditions of self-reliance in Chinese communities which, in a sense, allowed the needs of this group in society to be overlooked by the agencies responsible for the provision of services.

Following the publication of the report, the National Children's Home, Scotland, a voluntary organisation dedicated to the welfare of children and families in general, set up a study of the Chinese community in the Garnethill area of the city. As a result, the San Jai Chinese Project – the name derives from the Hakka and Cantonese pronunciation of Garnethill – was inaugurated in July 1985.

The San Jai Project was a partnership between Strathclyde Regional Council and the National Children's Home, the major source of funding being the latter. (Strathclyde Regional Council was dissolved in 1996).

The Project, which in 1991 moved from Hill Street to new premises in Rose Street, offers a very broad range of services to the Chinese community – from the provision of information and advice to support for many cultural activities.

The need for good support services for the Chinese community in Scotland as a

Like many Chinese in Glasgow, the Lees, among themselves, speak a language called Hakka, but most of the Chinese in Britain speak Cantonese. Another Chinese language is Mandarin, the language spoken in the north of China, and the country's official language. All these languages have only one written script, and this is the name 'Lee' written in Chinese.

whole was highlighted in 1990, when a major seminar was held in Glasgow. This seminar, entitled 'The Chinese Voice their Needs', looked closely at the needs of the community in matters of housing, health care, the lives of young people, and the welfare of the elderly. The seminar dealt with the 'myth' that assumed that Chinese people have less need of services than other parts of the population because of traditions of 'self-help', and emphasised that there were urgent needs which did require to be met – not least among them the need to confront the Chinese experiences of racism (see page 123).

Over the years, an increasing number of community organisations have been founded to support the Chinese population of Glasgow, such as the Kat-O Benevolent Society or the Wing Hong Elderly Group, which, with 400 members, is reputed to be the largest group of its kind in the United Kingdom.

The Glasgow branch of the Scotland China Association also offers support and friendship to a number of new migrants to be found in the city – some, for example, from mainland China, who have settled here in the wake of events in Tiananmen Square in Beijing in June 1989, and some former residents of Hong Kong, who have come to this country prior to

Chinese children in the San Jai Project in Hill Street.

Mr Jimmy Wong, January 1985, in his restaurant in Sauchiehall Street, with Constable Simon Keenan, at that time Gamethill's own policeman.

Picture by kind permission of the *Glasgow Herald*.

1997 and the return of the colony to China. As it has grown, the Scotland China Association has extended its activities to include the publication of a magazine – *Sine* – which in 2016 ran a schools art competition honouring a founder member, in the Tom Murray Memorial Prize. In June 2016 the association celebrated its 50th anniversary.

So, in Glasgow, while many Chinese are engaged in the catering business, there are also many others working in the professions: doctors, solicitors, university lecturers, and so on. This trend is growing, moreover, as young people born in this country of Chinese parents move outwith the traditional industries to work in the occupations of the wider community, or enter higher education.

The Chinese people can be Christian, Buddhist, or profess other religions or no particular religion. In another report, published in 1982, which looked at Chinese children in British schools, it was noted that

Chinese children celebrating the Chinese New Year on the stage of the Banqueting Hall in Glasgow City Chambers.

among Chinese born in Britain, there still remained a strong sense of 'being Chinese', and a respect for a cultural tradition stretching back 4,500 years.

In Glasgow, while the Chinese presence continues to be represented in restaurants and shops, such as the 1992 Chinatown development in the Dundas Vale area, there is also a thriving cultural and artistic life. A rich expression of this life is seen, year by year, in the

The Scotsman, 22 March 1990

Chinese voice their needs

BY SUSAN DEAN

Late night working in a hot food takeaway in Stirling can have fraught moments, according to 19-year-old twins Si Choi and Si Chianh Long.

Admittedly, it is not always like the time when a rowdy smashed the plateglass shop front but, say the girls, the funny thing is that the chip shop nearby in the same street does not appear to get quite the same level of hassle.

The girls, whose grandparents are Chinese, are not sure if the owner is English or Scottish but they point out that it is certainly not Chinese-owned and operated.

The twins talked about the difficulties they face when dozens of Chinese attended *The Chinese Voice Their Needs* seminar in Glasgow yesterday.

Maggie Chetty, Strathclyde senior community relations worker, reckons there can hardly be a Chinese food outlet in Scotland which has not experienced some form of racial abuse from the clientele.

Fear of retribution is widespread, and often the shop operators do not even bother to tell the police for the same reason, she says.

The seminar heard claims that Chinese in Scotland are losing out on access to public housing, social service and health provision, and employment opportunities because not enough is being done by local authorities to help Chinese avail themselves of all the opportunities.

Evening Times, 20 March 1990

CHINESE RACISM FIGHT

By NEIL GIBSON

SCOTLAND'S Chinese community was today urged to fight back against racism.

A major conference on the problems faced by Scotland's 20,000 Chinese is being held in Glasgow tomorrow.

Chinese activists from all over Scotland will attend the talk-in, which hopes to strengthen the Chinese community's fight for equality.

Conference chairman Chi Khen Pan, of the Scottish Chinese Steering Group, said today: "One of the myths still alive in Scotland is that racism and discrimination do not affect the Chinese community.

'We need to be more outspoken about harassment in Chinese restaurants and takeaways, and lack of access to other fields of employment.'

SCHEMES

The conference – The Chinese Voice Their Needs – will be held at the city's Mitchell Theatre.

Representatives from the Chinese community, along with professionals, will debate the lack of services, employment and welfare rights for Chinese people.

Mr Pan, a Strathclyde Community Relations Officer, continued: "Unless the Chinese community become more vociferous in demanding their rights, they are going to lose out in access to funding, job creation schemes and basic welfare rights.

Organisers hope the seminar will lead to local initiatives being started all over Scotland.

The Chinese School.

celebration of the important festival of Chinese New Year as it extends beyond that community to the city at large.

A vigorous and resourceful Chinese community continues to flourish in Glasgow at the present time. While the Census data for 2001 show no massive increase in numbers for the city as such, the figure for the West of Scotland is around 6,000, demonstrating that the community has moved out from its traditional hub in the Garnethill area of Glasgow. The majority of Chinese people in Scotland as a whole were born in the Far East – a third of the existing population born in this country.

When the end of the 99-year lease saw Hong Kong returned to China in 1997, it did produce a number of new immigrants, but now, in the 21st century, most of the new arrivals are young people coming from mainland China to study in the universities and colleges of the city. The Glasgow School of Art, for example, has joined forces with the Central Academy of Fine Arts in Beijing to offer students from China a new course in Glasgow, and 36 students enrolled in 2006.

The census information and the presence of students in the city show that the age profile of the Chinese community tends to be younger than that of the indigenous population. This is highlighted by the thriving Glasgow Chinese School.

The Glasgow Chinese School has operated for 34 years, starting from a small corps of less than 40 pupils to its present roll of almost 500. Students travel from all over the West of Scotland to study Cantonese or Mandarin. When the first Chinese School opened in 1973, it was aimed at preserving the language and culture for children born in Scotland.

This aim is well realised today in the school's permanent base in Stow College – as the Stow College Glasgow Chinese School. The institution is charitable and non-profit-making, and not only teaches language but also organises activities for parents while their children attend the Saturday language classes.

The headteacher of the school, Sam Chau, has lived in Scotland for many years. When Mr Chau came to Glasgow with his wife, Lin, they started a printing business, and were the first to bring Chinese typeset and computer fonts to Glasgow. Now Mr Chau is also manager of the Wing Ho Elderly Centre.

This centre has offered essential services to the elderly Chinese in Glasgow for a considerable number of years, but in 2005 the Wing Ho moved into a new home in a renovated B-listed building in Hill Street in Garnethill. The centre has 700 members, who are supported in many ways, providing a vital service against the isolation or cultural differences felt by some elderly Chinese. Of immense value is the Diabetic Clinic, run within the centre by the local doctor's practice, which has resolved many of the difficulties of access or language. The staff of the Wing Ho Centre also provide support with welfare benefits of every kind, including health advocacy, counselling and home support, besides general translation and interpreting.

Much of the Centre's activity, however, is recreational: members can enjoy a lunch club, English classes, computer classes, pottery and card games or exercise classes, besides shopping trips or outings in the Centre's own mini-bus. All of this has been richly enhanced by the new garden at the rear of the Hill Street premises.

The Chinese Garden was the product of a makeover by the BBC Beechgrove Garden team, with help and financial input from a range of

Sam Chau.

interested parties in addition to Glasgow City Council and Strathclyde Police. The Oriental-style garden, which has a pavilion and fountain, involved the support of the local community police officers, one of whom voiced the view that 'cultural projects that encourage interaction in the community help break down barriers and build bridges'. Another invaluable facility for the elderly Chinese of Glasgow is Wing Ho Court, a sheltered housing complex in Pitt Street.

The strength and the importance of the existing support for the Chinese community in Glasgow, old and young, was recognised when Sam Chau was honoured by the award of the MBE for his services to his community.

Chinese cultural life in general also flourishes in Glasgow – the China Scotland Association is still going strong, nurturing all aspects of Chinese life and culture, and holds regular meetings, talks, concerts and information events. The liaison officer for the China Scotland Association was Lin Chau, who, with her partner, Julia Hung, founded ricefield, the Chinese arts and cultural centre on West Graham Street.

Ricefield is the hub for Chinese arts and culture in Scotland. It was the Glasgow meeting point for Chinese artists, musicians and designers, providing a consultation service, workshops and classes on music, language, calligraphy and more. In July 2006 ricefield and the cultural centre were involved in 'Journey to The West: the Chinese Scottish Chronicles', which charted the passage of the Chinese to Scotland over time. Photographs, exhibits, text and a short film told the history of the Scottish Chinese. The centre moved to much expanded premises, in Baltic Chambers, Wellington Street, in Glasgow.

History and tradition were the focus of the 'One Million Days in China' exhibition at the Burrell Collection in 2005, which ended with a major celebration of Chinese New Year. Emma Leighton, curator of Chinese and Oriental Civilisations at the Collection, described the exhibition as 'an amazing celebration of Chinese culture in Glasgow', as the exhibition brought contact with Chinese youth groups, the elderly centre, the Chinese School and the Chinese Christian Church.

The community has also kept in touch with events by a free periodical – the *Chinese Community News* – produced by the Chinese Community Development Partnership (CCDP), based in the West End of the city. The CCDP remains active in many areas and in 2006 was nominated for the Pearl Awards for outstanding service to the community. The CCDP organises many community-based activities; for example, supporting those who attended a seminar run in Glasgow by the International Organisation for Migration to inform about the 'Enhanced Reintegration Assistance Scheme'. This was a new programme run by the Home Office and the European Union to assist those who may wish to return to their home countries. The CCDP also organises recreational activities, such as outings or projects involving the Dragonet Youth Club.

With the Chinese Students and Scholars Association, the Glasgow Chinese Women's Group, the Glasgow Oriental Dancing Association, the various outlets for Chinese medicine, the Active Life hill-walking club, and the Glasgow Chinese Healthy Living Centre – this last which held a Sports and Fun Day in Kelvin Hall in August 2006, which covered yoga, Tai Chi, table tennis, basketball, football, badminton and a host of other activities – the community is well served with recreational activities.

The Kut-O Buddhist Association is still active in the city, as is the colourful mall of stores in Chinatown at Dundas Vale, and many other Chinese businesses.

In January 2004, the second China Scotland Film Festival was launched to coincide with the Chinese New Year. The then Culture Minister of the Scottish Government, Frank McAveety, in opening the festival at the Centre for Contemporary Arts, said:

> The festival signifies the contribution that Chinese culture plays in today's Scotland. Its impact is around us, influences us, educates us about Chinese tradition and fosters lasting friendships and understanding.

The abundance of Chinese life in Glasgow today, as described above, must serve to confirm McAveety's words. The Chinese community, in no uncertain terms, belongs to Glasgow now. For a number of years, moreover, Glasgow City Council has been twinned with the city of Dalian, the most northerly coastal city in China. This relationship, together with the new China–Scotland initiative promoted by the Scottish Government, will ensure that Glasgow's Chinese connections will continue to develop and thrive. Particularly since the most recent Census for Glasgow City highlighted an increase in the Chinese population from 3,876 in 2001 to 10,689 in 2011.

A significant development in Scotland/China relationships was the founding of SCEN, in 2006. SCEN is the Scotland China Education Network. It exists to promote learning of Chinese and about China itself in Scottish schools, bringing together individuals, national agencies and associations keen to further teaching and learning. In 2006 the Scottish Government welcomes SCEN as part of Scotland's Strategy for Stronger Engagement with China. SCEN supported all national agencies in their plans to introduce Chinese to the curriculum, brought practitioners together to share expertise and good practice through network meetings and provided a platform for pupils to present their learning at SCEN pupil conferences. The fourth SCEN Youth Summit was held in 2015.

SCEN was established as a voluntary association with its own governing body, and its convener, Dr Judith McClure, is a member of the Scottish Schools Advisory Group on China set up in 2010, and has been appointed Ambassador for the teaching of Chinese in Scottish schools at the Confucius Institute for Scotland at Edinburgh University.

CHAPTER 8

The Asian Community

THE LARGEST GROUP of people who made Glasgow their home in the second half of the 20th century was made up of Indians, Pakistanis and Bangladeshis: collectively referred to as Asians. In explaining the use of this term, the Runnymede Trust points out that it is

> commonly used to describe persons born in India or Pakistan, or to descendants of such persons who were born in East Africa who subsequently migrated to the United Kingdom. It is also used to refer to children born in the United Kingdom of both groups. When used it should be recognised that it refers to a wide range of people.

Today, many younger people or children born in Glasgow to parents of Indian or Pakistani origin might see themselves as Asian, but, most positively, also see themselves as British and, in some cases, Asian Scots.

In a series of articles in a newssheet entitled the *Gorbals View*, published in 1967, a member of the Pakistani community traced the early history of Indian settlement in Glasgow, and identified the first immigrant, about whom much is known, as Noor Muhammad Tanda. Mr Tanda left Bombay in 1916 at the age of 19 and travelled to Britain, arriving at Liverpool. He moved on to Glasgow and lived in lodgings in the Broomielaw until he found work in a Greenock shipyard. Later, Mr Tanda left Scotland and travelled extensively, even spending five years in Australia, where his father was living, but he returned and settled down again in Glasgow in the 1930s when he became part of a business in the Gorbals which was to trade for many years under the name Tanda, Ashrif and Company.

While Mr Tanda may have been notable as one of the earliest Asian residents of Glasgow, he was not unusual in having left India to settle elsewhere: there was already a long tradition of movement from the subcontinent to other parts of the world. Sometimes, people left India to seek opportunity abroad, but more often they were forced by circumstances beyond their control – famine, poverty or disease, or in answer to pressure from Britain to provide labour in other British colonies throughout the world.

British influence in India began as early as 1600, when Queen Elizabeth I granted a charter to the East India Company to trade with India. For centuries, India had traded overland with Europe and China but it was the Portuguese who first opened up a sea route to the sub-continent. It was dislike of the Portuguese by the Indians which gave the British East India Company the opportunity to take the immensely profitable Indian trade away from the Portuguese. Similar trading companies had been formed by other European countries and the competition was fierce, but the most successful were the British and the French. Eventually, the British defeated the French and remained as the sole foreign power with influence in India. As this power grew, one Indian historian points out 'the British, who came to trade, remained to rule over the whole of India' (Majundar and Copra, *Main Currents of Indian History*).

This was still some time away and in the earliest days British influence was limited to several areas around Bombay, Madras and Calcutta. In 1668, however, when the East India Company rented Bombay *for ever* from Charles II, it was decreed that from that date people born in Bombay were to be 'natural subjects' of Great Britain. A similar decree had been enacted in Barbados in 1605, and it was from such beginnings that the principle of overseas British subjects arose.

India was a land rich in spices, tea, precious minerals and luxury textiles. The East India Company set out to trade but was always anxious to extend British power abroad. This was achieved in India by exploiting the internal divisions in Indian society which already existed between the rich and powerful princely states. The Mughal Empire, which had dominated the sub-continent for over 300 years, was in a weakened condition. Independent states fought each other for supremacy while the people suffered. The British adopted a policy of 'divide and rule' by supporting one state against another, with Indian armies recruited and trained by the British. Historians acknowledge that 'Indian regiments did most of the work in conquering India for the English' (Kiernan, *Lords of Human Kind*).

By the end of the 18th century, Britain controlled most of India, but during the 19th century Indian hostility to British rule grew. British policy was to 'westernise' the administration of India, in law, in language, and with English-style education and English personnel in all high offices. Indians were denied important posts in administration and were frequently treated with contempt by British officials. Englishmen brought up to be proud of Britain's rapid industrial progress were expected to promote 'the

British way of life' in the colonies, and it was not difficult for them to ignore the poverty created by British economic policy in India: as we have seen, Victorian Britain had its share of poverty and squalor too. British 'superiority' was based in steamships, railways, weapons and the manufacturing industry, and in protecting British manufacture and exports Indian trade and industry suffered greatly. Britain took Indian raw materials such as cotton (particularly after the American Civil War cut off that source of supply) and exported manufactured goods back to India, to be sold more cheaply than the Indians could sell their own goods. The unhappy position of the Indian economy and the insensitive nature of much British rule led to an eruption of Indian feeling in what the British know as 'The Indian Mutiny' and Indians refer to as 'The Great Revolt', when the Bengal Army rose against its British masters in 1857. It has been said that

> the soldiers, and to some extent the country as a whole were suffering from a divided soul – the uprising a measure of the tensions created by British rule.
>
> *New Cambridge Modern History*

The revolt shocked the British government and was to be the dividing line between two distinct periods of British rule in India, changing what had been basically a trading empire into a military one with an army of occupation whose duty was to assist in maintaining British rule. Part of the justification for this was the British belief that they brought the blessings of 'order and justice' into societies that were incapable of looking after themselves. Allied to this was the desire to spread Christian belief among people whose own religious traditions, art, philosophy and literature were already founded in an ancient civilisation. The British, who believed that they had a moral duty to eradicate some of the practices of Indian society which they found contradictory to Christian ideas, did not respect this ancient civilisation and culture. After the uprising of 1857, India was ruled from London, and millions of Indians became subjects of the British crown. India was becoming known as the richest possession in the expanding British Empire – 'the jewel in the crown' – and a speech given by Professor Ruskin in Oxford in 1870 was typical of the beliefs of many people in Britain. He argued that the British should

> found colonies as far and as fast as she is able, formed of her most energetic and worthiest men – seizing every piece of fruitful waste ground she can set foot on, and there teaching those her colonists

that their chief virtue is to be fidelity to their country and that their first aim is to advance the power of England by land and sea.

In advancing the power of England, many Indians found themselves as seamen on British ships, soldiers in British armies, or as the cheap labour who built railways, canals and dams in British colonies throughout the world. Even at this early date, a few of these men found their way to Britain.

In 1873, Joseph Salter, 'Missionary to the Wandering Asiatics of England', found

at this point about 250 Asiatics... were constantly visiting the provincial towns... wander from Plymouth to Ben Lomond and from Aberdeen to Hastings.

Salter noted that some of these men were found in Glasgow in 1869. These were probably the forerunners of the Indian pedlars who were common in Scotland in the early 20th century – some may once have been seamen on British vessels, like those seen by that ever-observant Glasgow writer who described the Jews and Italians in such colourful terms:

... close on the heels... come several swarthy sons of India. They are members of the crew of some East Indiaman lying in the docks. The evening being warm their usually shivering aspect has disappeared and their sable faces glisten with delight.

Hammerton, *Sketches from Glasgow*

The writer's attitude to the Indians, and to the other foreigners whom he met on his walks through Glasgow, was typical of the way in which all foreigners were regarded by a section of British society at the time. Anyone who was not British was seen as perhaps exotic, but certainly inferior, and unimportant enough to be described in careless or unfavourable terms. This was no more than a reflection of how the British treated most foreigners, even when the Briton was himself the foreigner in other countries.

In the 1880s the Indian National Congress was set up to give the Indian people a voice. After the tremendous service in the First World War of the Indian soldiers and seamen, the British government conceded that it would consider the question of Indian self-government. The Government of India Act in 1919 did grant a measure of self-government to the subcontinent, but it was not enough – and how little it meant was brought home when the army massacred hundreds of Indians engaged in a peaceful demonstration at Amritsar on 1 April 1919. By 1920–1, the popular agitation for Home Rule had become a mass movement. Under the leadership of Mahatma Gandhi and M. A. Jinnah, the Indians struggled for many years before achieving their goal of total independence of British rule.

In the aftermath of the Second World War, independence was gained in 1947. Once again, India and other colonies had provided massive forces on the British side, the Indian people had faced threats of invasion from South-East Asia, and also experienced the deprivation and sacrifice which was the cost of the struggle to preserve Western-style democracy. In the light of these experiences, the notion that people should fight in the name of democracy while dominating others became morally indefensible.

In August 1947, when the sub-continent of India was partitioned into the two separate countries of India and Pakistan, there was a small number of Indians living and working in Glasgow. The 1914 Imperial Act had finalised the principle that 'everyone born within the allegiance of the crown in any part of the Empire was a British subject', and was therefore, by right, free to live in any part of the Empire, including Britain. Some of these people, like Mr Tanda, had been settled for some time and were part of a small community that had developed in the 1930s. The first wholesale warehouse had opened in 1929, mainly to supply stock to door-to-door salesmen, and the first grocer's shop opened in 1930. In 1936–7, the first children, boys, had come to join their fathers, and had entered Buchan Street Primary School in the Gorbals; one of these boys, M. Ibrahim Ashrif, was later to gain his Doctor of Philosophy from Edinburgh University and was subsequently awarded the MBE for his work in this country. Several small businesses had been started by the time war came in 1939. A few of the settlers went back to India, some joined the armed forces, and the rest went to work in factories producing war materials. It is estimated that at this time there were about 50 members in the Glasgow Indian community.

This small group had grown to about 100 by August 1947, most living in the Gorbals area. Some were Hindu in religion and some were Sikh – the first Sikh temple in Glasgow existed in 1911 – but the majority were, then as now, Muslims. In the early days in the city, the Muslim residents hired a billiard hall in Oxford Street for the Friday prayers, and in 1944 the Muslim Mission bought the property and converted it into a mosque and hall for the use of the Muslim community in Glasgow – the first mosque in all of Scotland.

On 15 August 1947, the day after the division of the Indian subcontinent, India attained its independence from British rule. In India, the Muslim League had argued for a separate state for Muslims, and Pakistan was created. In Glasgow, the Asian community celebrated the new era, but their joy was shortlived. Pakistan had a strong Hindu and Sikh minority and the new independent India had a large Muslim population. Soon after independence these minorities began to migrate on a massive scale across the new border to escape from the inevitable persecution. As Hindus and Sikhs migrated from Pakistan to India and millions of Muslims moved from India to Pakistan, massive riots and the mass murders of bus and trainloads of migrants resulted in enormous loss of life on both sides.

The disruption in India and Pakistan, however, coincided with a period of post-war labour shortage in Britain, and many Asians who had lost homes, jobs or businesses in the upheaval were encouraged to come to Britain.

This was emphasised by the passing of the British Nationality Act in 1948, which granted UK citizenship to people of Britain's colonies or former colonies. From 1948 to 1953 almost all the immigrants who came were people who had been affected by the partitioning of the subcontinent, and who were made welcome by statements such as that of James Callaghan MP, who stressed the need for 'an addition to our population which only immigration can provide'.

Many of the Asians who began to arrive in the 1950s, mainly from the Punjab, were from an agricultural background, but when they came to Britain they worked in textile mills and factories, and on public transport, often working long, unsocial hours in jobs that the native population did not want. Research has shown that there was an exact correlation between post-war immigration from the countries of the New Commonwealth and unfilled vacancies in the United Kingdom. This was true of Glasgow, when many of the immigrants earned their first money and laid the foundations of the savings that would later be put into homes and small businesses, by working for Glasgow Corporation Transport. The transport system was then desperately short of staff. The wages were quite good for the time but the shifts worked made the job unpopular at a time when there was no shortage of other work in the city, and so the transport department was pleased to welcome the extra labour provided by the immigrants.

Most of those who came at first were men, who usually lived in groups while they saved enough to provide for wives and children when they could eventually join them. Sometimes this took as long as eight years of hard work and careful saving. By about 1960, it is estimated that there were about 3,000 Asians in Glasgow, and a start had been made in setting up community organisations. In 1955, the Indian Film Society had begun and in the same year the Pakistani Social and Cultural Society was also set up.

Working together for Glasgow and Glasgow Corporation Transport.
Photograph by kind permission of Scottish International Labour Council.

In 1962, the first Immigration Act was passed, designed to restrict the numbers of people entering Britain to live. After 1962, therefore, most of the people arriving from India and Pakistan, or Asians from the former British possessions in East Africa, were the families and dependants of those who were already settled here. In Glasgow, early Asian settlement was concentrated for the most part in the Gorbals, Govanhill, Pollokshields, and later, Woodside. Despite the 1962 Act, the number of Asians in the city was still growing because people moved within Britain, and some were coming from the Midlands or other parts of England, particularly some of those who came to work on the transport system. Some of these were younger people, with a good command of English – an asset for work on the trams or buses.

A survey carried out in the city in 1971 suggested that there were by this time around 12,000 people of Asian origin living in Glasgow. During

GLASGOW CORPORATION TRANSPORT

VACANCIES FOR:-
- ## BUS DRIVERS
- ## CONDUCTORS
- ## CONDUCTRESSES

ONLY PERSONS OF GOOD CHARACTER NEED APPLY

WAGES AND CONDITIONS

AVERAGE WEEKLY EARNINGS   (excluding overtime)

DRIVERS   199/- rising to 202/- after one year

CONDUCTORS } 193/- rising to 196/- after one year
CONDUCTRESSES }

An advertisement for Glasgow Corporation Transport.

this time, the Gorbals was becoming more or less evacuated for slum clearance and reconstruction and the Asians, like others, were moving out. The survey was interested to see where Asians chose to live, and if they preferred to live near each other rather than be scattered throughout the community. The researchers found that Asians usually moved into fairly old tenement property, which they bought: Asian people prefer to own their homes rather than rent them and, in any case, at this time few would have qualified for local authority housing.

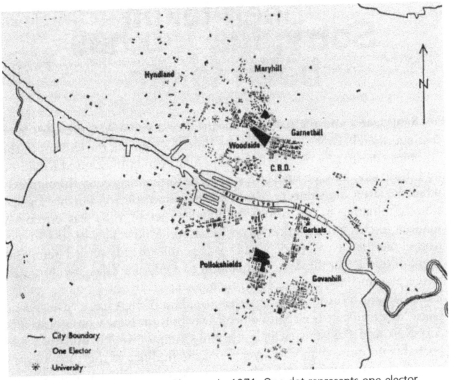

The Asian communities in Glasgow in 1971. One dot represents one elector.
From *Scottish Geographical*, 1971.

Later, in 1977, another survey carried out in the city looked at the fortunes of those young people, many who were by this time the Scottish-born children of Asian parents, when it came to finding employment. The research suggested that life in Glasgow was not always easy for these young Glaswegians who, even though they were products of the same education system as their white contemporaries, found it harder to get work or to enter apprenticeships, outside family- or Asian-owned businesses.

This situation was not improved by the general rise in youth unemployment in the years that followed and young Asians found that frequently, despite good qualifications, they had a harder task finding work than their white peers.

New Society 28 April 1977

Sorry, the job has been taken

Bridget Fowler, Barbara Littlewood and Ruth Madigan

Even if Asian school-leavers have high hopes of getting professional jobs, they may nonetheless end up working within their own community.

New Society, 28 April 1977.

Since 1968 and the Commonwealth Immigrants Act, the laws have distinguished between citizens of the United Kingdom, the citizens of the colonies who have a parent or grandparent born in the United Kingdom and those who have no such ancestors. The former may enter Britain freely while the latter are subject to strict immigration control. Further legislation culminating in the British Nationality Act of 1981 has effectively reduced further immigration from India and Pakistan, with the exception of families, wives or dependants of people already settled here. One result of this is that the Asian population of a city like Glasgow does not, at the present time, change very much. A report by the Commission for Racial Equality estimated that the population increase in 1981–6 in Glasgow of those whose family head was born in New Commonwealth countries and Pakistan (which left the Commonwealth in 1972) was probably no more than 500 a year, and the findings of the 1991 Census would confirm this, since the figures for those identified as representing the Asian communities in the City of Glasgow indicate that the total population has grown to little more than 15,000.

The largest number of Asians settled in Scotland originates from the West Punjab, which is in Pakistan, and East Punjab, which is in India. Though Urdu is the national language of Pakistan and Hindi the national language of India, the most commonly spoken language among Asians in Glasgow is Punjabi. Today, besides Urdu and Punjabi, other Asian languages are taught in several secondary schools in Glasgow, and bilingual teachers are employed in a number of primary schools to give

Racial equality update

We want to hear from black people . . .

THE term "Ethnic Minority" is often used to identify members of the community who are subjected to racism. I prefer to use the term "black". I offer my apologies to anyone I offend by choosing this term.

You may have read in the April issue of Strathclyde Report that the Regional Council have agreed a "Racial Equality" policy.

The policy includes the issues of Employment, Training, Cultural Diversity, Communication, Partnership and Accountability.

So we want to hear from black people in Strathclyde about their hopes and needs.

Particularly about the kinds of employment they seek and what difficulties they face.

In Scotland there is a widely held belief that black people, especially young black people, do not have the same employment hopes as young white people.

It is said that Asian youngsters will be given jobs either in their father's shop or in a restaurant.

Even if this notion were true, many cornershops are for a variety of reasons having to close.

Each closure is one less job chance for you if you are unemployed and black.

Have you faced racial discrimination at any point? Please let us know.

A plea from the Strathclyde report for information from young black people about their experiences of racial discrimination.

mother-tongue support in the early stages. Strathclyde Regional Council continued to support the further recruitment of personnel from the Asian community, in education and other departments, and in addition, the regional and district councils have instituted departments specifically charged with matters of racial equality.

Books, records and video films in the languages of the Asian community have also become more readily available over the years, as have daily and weekly newspapers – some produced in Britain but others imported from the subcontinent. Much of the literary material was available in the first Asian bookshop to be opened in Scotland, which is also situated in the South Side of Glasgow, and some of the Glasgow City

Libraries also stock a range of materials in the various languages of the communities.

The Asian community in Glasgow also supports a number of leisure and recreational activities, including several sports. There are clubs and groups for most ages but the provision is not enough to meet all the needs of the population. The Scottish Asian Action Committee, an 'umbrella' organisation representing the various interests of the Asian population, is a federation of such bodies as the Asian Artistes Association, the Bangladesh Association, the Indian Association, the Sikh Sabha, and many more.

Today, besides the traditional Asian businesses such as restaurants, stores and warehouses, Glasgow Asians are to be found in public life and in the professions of law, medicine, accountancy, teaching, and so on. As second- or even third-generation children grow up in Glasgow, they are choosing to go into the new industries and the professions to a far greater extent than before, and are less willing to follow in their parents' footsteps in their choice of a career.

For some Asians, living or growing up in Glasgow has had a powerful effect upon them, and has led them to identify closely with the city and to regard it with some affection. One such Glasgow Asian is Gurmeet Mattu, who gave his 'Personal View of Glasgow' in the bulletin of Strathclyde Community Relations Council, *Community Voice*. Of his home, he had this to say: 'The future holds no fear for me, I'm happy in my city state.' Gurmeet Mattu goes on to suggest that Glasgow is a friendly city with little dark spots of racial discrimination best left unexplored, but other opinion, and a growing body of evidence, suggests that his is a minority view. Other Asians argue that racial abuses and harassment are becoming more frequent elements of life in Glasgow, and various official and press reports confirm this view, including, for example, the series of reports by the *Daily Record* and Scottish Television in 1990. In the same year, all staff in Strathclyde schools were issued with a statement of the authority's policy in the area and guidelines for tackling racist incidents in schools. Education, housing, social work and police departments also meet in multi-agency racial incident groups in several parts of the city.

The council has also been involved for a number of years in the provision of a range of projects designed to improve service delivery to the minority ethnic communities – in social welfare, community education, the arts, and so on – all of this basic to the philosophy expressed in the authority's stance on racial equality and equal opportunities. Referring

An example of the many Asian shops serving the community in Glasgow.

to harassment and discrimination, Kaliani Lyle, a member of the Asian community working in race relations in Scotland, noted:

> Black people can know facts of injustice for years but they are not real until white research validates them.
> *Church of Scotland Working Party Report*, 1990

Ultimately, as the previous chapters have demonstrated, Glasgow's traditional reputation for friendliness has been heavily dependent, for the incomer, on an ability to blend into the surroundings with the minimum of protest: to present no 'threat' either in religious or economic terms, and eventually to become indistinguishable from other Glaswegians. When all that has come to pass, Glasgow is, for you, the friendly city of repute. However, if you are a Glasgow Asian, it is argued, the route to equality will have to be found in continued vigilance and positive action – educational, political and social – rather than in some kind of partial and unwelcome assimilation. Only then can you say, with some chance of meaning it, 'I belong to Glasgow'.

The 2001 Census in Scotland showed the Asian population of Greater Glasgow to be in excess of 30,000. By far the biggest group had a Pakistani background, with those of Indian origin the second largest. For the first time in 2001, the census asked a question about ethnic identity, and this is reflected in the figures.

The Asian presence in Glasgow is very well established – with community organisations in abundance. The *Ethnic Minority Directory* of Glasgow City Council lists more than 160 organisations that provide relevant services in the city. Some of these are long-standing, such the Mel-Milaap Centre and the Garnethill Multicultural Community Centre. Since 1984, there has also been the Islamic Centre, which has a wide social, educational and cultural remit in respect of the Muslim community. At the time of the earthquake in Pakistan in 2005, while help went out from all sectors of society, the compassion and generosity of the city's Pakistani community was boundless. Much of this aid was coordinated by the Glasgow Islamic Society. The Muslim population is also served by the *iwitness*, a free newspaper distributed to the Muslim communities of Glasgow, Edinburgh, Dundee and Aberdeen. In July 2006 the paper interviewed Bashir Ahmad, with the headline 'Scotland prepares for its first non-white MSP'. Mr Ahmad was elected to the Scottish Parliamentary elections in May 2007, for the Scottish National Party (SNP). Alex Salmond, leader of the SNP, described Bashir Ahmad's success as 'a new dawn' in Scottish politics.

Mr Ahmad, who has since died, was typical of many who came from Pakistan as a young man, worked in public transport then went into business. He had been President of the Pakistani Welfare Association on a number of occasions and in 1995 formed Scottish Asians for Independence, with the aim of building support for the SNP within the Asian community.

On a different side of the political perspective, of course, was the highly respected and extremely well-known Labour Member of Parliament, Mohammad Sarwar.

Mohammad Sarwar, who was born in Pakistan in 1952, holds a BA in Political Science, English and Urdu, and was for many years a successful businessman before going into politics. He was MP for Govan from 1997 – and held the Glasgow Central seat for Labour since the 2005 general election. When he entered Parliament in 1997, Mohammad Sarwar was the first ethnic minority MP in Scotland, and the first ever Muslim MP in the United Kingdom.

The list of Glasgow Asians who have become successful in their chosen field is long indeed, but among the best-known young entrepreneurs must be Charan Gill and Sanjay Mahju. Charan Gill published his autobiography in 2006, aptly named *Tikka Look at Me Now*. In 2005, Charan Gill's New Harlequin business empire, the Spice of Life and the well-known Ashoka brand restaurants in the city, was taken over by Sanjay Mahju. Sanjay now runs 16 restaurants with 350 staff.

Sanjay Mahju, son of a Hindu father and Sikh mother, has lived in Glasgow since the age of two. When he was a child, the family spent some time in East Kilbride, where he experienced the discomfort of being the only Asian in his class. But all of that changed when he moved back to Glasgow and to a school on the South Side. In an interview, Sanjay said:

The minute I walked into Cuthbertson Primary... I saw it was full of Chinese, African and Asian kids and I fitted in for the first time in years.

Evening Times, 31 March 2005

The place of the community in the Scottish educational environment was confirmed in the recent report that Urdu will be taught for the Scottish Higher Certificate. This has been achieved after a sustained campaign by Asian parents and Shawlands Academy, a secondary school on the South Side of the city, almost half of whose pupils are from Asian backgrounds. The Scottish Qualifications Authority introduced the new Higher Qualification from August 2007. It is a mark of the community's settled presence that Urdu is the first non-European language to be recognised at this level, though Standard Grade Urdu has been available since 1994.

A former pupil of Shawlands Academy who is making his mark on the cultural scene is Atta Yacub, leading man in the successful films *Ae Fond Kiss*, in 2004, and *Nina's Heavenly Delights*, in 2006. Atta Yacub was born in Glasgow in 1979, and has been referred to as 'a Scotsman very much in touch with his Asian roots'. Atta is more than a film actor. His CV includes a degree in IT Management and he continued to work with the Youth Counselling Services Agency in Pollokshields, where he grew up. This work took him mountaineering and canoeing with underprivileged children.

Today, the Asian community in Glasgow is extremely diverse, and a

Atta Yacub.
Photo courtesy of Robert Perry, *Scotsman* Newspapers.

little of that has been shown above. Mohammed Sarwar, Sanjay Mahju and Atta Yacub are very public individuals, but there are many other Asians, in business, education, medicine, the law and other professions, who find Glasgow a satisfactory place to live, work and raise their families, while giving back to the city in countless ways, and may well be happy to say, like Atta Yacub, 'I'm Glasgow through and through'.

* * *

It is to be hoped that Atta Yacub's outlook remains that of most Asians in Glasgow and beyond in 2016.

In 2011 The National Records of Scotland showed that there were 141,000 Asians in Scotland as a whole, some 35,000 of whom lived in Glasgow. The majority were of Pakistani origin, 22,405 while those of Indian extraction numbered 8,640, with a much smaller Bangladeshi group of 458. These figures were considerably higher than those of the 2001 Census, achieved not so much by immigration these days as by growing numbers of Asian Scots by birth still describing their ethnic origins as Asian in the Census question.

In any case, Scots Asians are deeply embedded in the culture, politics and business of Scotland and Glasgow in particular. Humza Yusaf, Scottish Nationalist Minister in the new Scottish government for example, chose to take his loyal oath in Urdu at the opening of parliament in May 2016. And in 2015, Tasmina Ahmed-Sheikh took her place in the House of Commons as an SNP MP.

Humza Yusaf.

Tasmina was also the founder of the Scottish Asian Women's Association, and is a partner in the Glasgow law firm, Hamilton Burns.

In business there are virtually too many successful Asian entrepreneurs to list, such as Afzal and Akmal Kitushi, who in 2003 were named as Scotland's richest Asian businessmen when they took over Trespass, the successful outdoor clothing company, and Munawar Sher, of the iconic Sher Cash and Carry business. More recently House of Sher Plaza has opened as the first Asian shopping mall. Based in Wallace Street in the south side of Glasgow, the mall boasts 40 stores and an Asian supermarket, Food Asia. Each year in fact, successful Asian businessmen and women are celebrated at an awards dinner in a Glasgow hotel.

Also on the south side is what the Scotsman newspaper described in July 2013 to be Scotland's most ethnically diverse street, in Albert Drive, Pollokshields. 'On the east side, home to the Tramway Theatre, Pollokshields East railway station and churches including Scotland's first purpose-built Sikh temple, and more Asian shops than you might find in an entire city elsewhere...'

Sikh Sabha, Berkeley Street.
Courtesy of David Cameron Photography.

The Sikh temple in Pollokshields, is not the only purpose-built temple in Glasgow, since the vast new Gurdwara Singh Sabha in Berkeley Street opened its doors for the first time in May 2016. The Muslim community has now no less than 28 mosques in Glasgow and its surrounding towns, while the Hindu presence is in the Hindu Mandir in La Belle Place. In May 2010 the temple was damaged in a severe blaze. The building, which in 2006 had opened as the biggest Hindu place of worship in Scotland, did not extend to other buildings in the area and was subsequently restored.

CHAPTER 9

Asylum Seekers

'WE RUN AWAY from unfairness, we run away from trouble, we run away from injustice, killing, inhumanity, where yes is no and no is yes – to Britain, to fairness, to warmth, to security.' These are the opening words spoken by Ahlam Souidi in a film made by the Scottish Refugee Council in 2005, intended to give insight into the lives of asylum seekers in Glasgow. There are almost 6,000 asylum seekers in Glasgow, from countries all over the world.

Asylum seekers and refugees come to the United Kingdom under the terms of the 1951 Refugee Convention. This convention was first legally defined by international agreement after the Second World War and was necessary to deal with the reality of thousands of people displaced from home and country.

The United Nations Refugee Convention, adopted in 1951, says that no-one must be sent back to a country where they would be at risk of persecution, on the grounds of race, religion, nationality, political opinion, or membership of a particular group. Thus, the convention defines as a refugee someone who is outside their country of origin because of a well-founded fear of persecution in that country, for any of the reasons outlined above.

Since 1951 there have been many different human rights agreements. Among these, and of particular relevance to refugees and asylum seekers in Britain, is the European Convention on Human Rights, which has been effective in the United Kingdom since 2000. Some of the rights contained in this convention are:

the right to life;
the right not to be tortured or treated in an inhuman or degrading way;
the right to be free from slavery or forced labour;
the right to liberty; and
the right to a fair trial.

Within the United Kingdom an asylum seeker is an individual who has applied for protection from the government for reasons of persecution or ill-treatment in their country of origin, and is waiting for the Home Office to make a decision on their application to remain in this country.

A refugee, on the other hand, is an asylum seeker whose claim for asylum has been accepted, and they are given 'leave to remain' in the United Kingdom. This is granted with an immigration status document issued by the Home Office to those foreign nationals who qualify for settlement or permanent residence: a UK Residence Permit. Until recently, this was granted as limited/indefinite leave to remain.

Asylum claimants can make a claim at their port of entry, to the Immigration and Nationality Directorate Office, or as soon after arrival as possible. The asylum seeker is required to show evidence of persecution under the 1951 Convention. Every new asylum seeker is issued with an Application Registration Card – a secure document that confirms evidence of the holder's identity. The National Asylum Support Service (NASS) then becomes responsible for supporting destitute asylum seekers and may provide financial support and/or accommodation. NASS also operates the dispersal system that brings asylum seekers to Glasgow, among other places, when the pressure on London and the South East becomes too great. NASS in turn makes the decision as to where asylum seekers will be located. Since 2000, Glasgow City Council has been the only local authority in Scotland to have accepted an agreed quota of asylum seekers.

When refugee status has been granted, indefinite leave to remain means that an individual is free to take paid employment and access higher education and other benefits available to UK citizens. This is currently being reconsidered by the Home Office, however, with new legislation planned which will change residential permission to five years, after which time the claimant's case will be reviewed and a new decision made in the light of circumstances in the country from which the refugee fled.

The asylum seeker does not have even this slender degree of security. Since an Act of Parliament in 2002, they may not take paid employment or enter into higher education, and must live on the benefits provided by central government funding to local councils.

The fairly short history of asylum seekers and refugees in Glasgow has been extremely varied, from loneliness, isolation and victimisation on the one hand, to the strenuous efforts made by individuals and groups to improve the lives of these men, women and children who have found themselves guests of the city through no choice of their own.

In 2000, when dispersal of asylum seekers began, many were housed by the council in empty flats in the north of the city. With no preparation for either the existing residents or the asylum seekers, Kurds, Iranians, Afghans and refugees from the Balkans found themselves living cheek by jowl, and there was much publicity at that time about the unfortunate scenario that had been created.

Almost immediately, Glasgow the Caring City, a charity group formed by local churches, swung into action to provide support, running centres in six parishes, in which the asylum seekers found language classes and even clothing. The YMCA were also involved when they took over one of the tower blocks on Red Road in Springburn, where many asylum seekers were living, and refurbished it.

As part of Caring City, the church minister, Edward Jones, and his wife, Elspeth, worked with the asylum seekers and both were awarded an MBE for their services to race and community relations. They said of the asylum seekers: 'They came in huge droves seeking help and we provided what we could.' Many of them highly educated, at least 12 of the people the Jones worked with were qualified doctors. Often they faced suspicion and outright hostility from the local community.

For all the good work of the churches and such individuals, life for the asylum seeker in Glasgow can be far from rosy. In July 2005, when the G8 countries were meeting in Perthshire to discuss world poverty, asylum seekers and refugees were telling their stories to the Glasgow *Evening Times*.

Khadija Coll, a Somali-born development officer with the African and Caribbean Network, spoke of how African refugees were struggling to find work in the face of rising levels of racism. People who had fled war zones in the hope of a better life were facing 'poverty, fear and racism'. Jobs were hard to come by for those Africans who were free to work, in spite of good qualifications. Robina Qureshi, of Positive Action on Housing, echoed these sentiments, saying that racism was 'a fact of their daily lives as asylum seekers or refugees' (*Evening Times*, 2 July 2005).

A survey by the Scottish Refugee Council, discussed by the *Evening Times*, revealed the number of well-qualified people who were living as asylum seekers in Glasgow – 70 per cent were from professional backgrounds and 75 per cent spoke more than one language – who were banned from taking paid employment.

As early as 2003, Glasgow City Council was lobbying the Home Office to allow skilled asylum seekers to work, in an effort to combat the worsening skills shortages. The pleas fell on deaf ears, since by the end of 2006 the council was still trying to make its case.

Many asylum issues have been given priority by organisations that have developed strategies to help asylum seekers and refugees, such as Oxfam Scotland. The work of this body continues to be extensive. A report in 2000, as asylum seekers first arrived in Glasgow, entitled 'Asylum', analysed the very negative coverage in certain organs of the popular press regarding asylum issues. The report was seriously concerned about the degree to which asylum seekers arriving in this country were demonised, creating a climate of fear and hostility among sections of the public.

In 1995, Oxfam had established the UK Poverty Programme and as part of that work has provided financial assistance and other forms of support for a number of projects supporting the short-term needs of asylum seekers. Importantly, Oxfam is seriously engaged at any time in a range of activities to improve existing knowledge about the circumstances of asylum seekers and refugees, change public and official attitudes and influence government policy. Oxfam is part of the Asylum Positive Images Network. Negative myths about asylum seekers, encouraged by the less scrupulous organs of the press and sometimes by political parties, are examined by Oxfam and bodies like the Convention of Scottish Local Authorities (COSLA).

At the end of 1999 COSLA set up the Refugee and Asylum Seeker Consortium (CRASC): this had the express remit of managing and monitoring the commissioning and provision of accommodation and other services to asylum seekers. Their website is a rich source of information for both refugees and migrant workers. An additional function of CRASC was the integration of refugees. A COSLA report in May 2005, by the Fraser of Allander Institute, was entitled 'The Impact of Asylum Seekers on the Glasgow Economy'. The research demonstrated that it was to Scotland's advantage to encourage asylum seekers, once they became refugees, to stay here with their skills and qualifications. It made the point that many asylum seekers are young and university educated, and that most of them, on gaining residential status, would wish to remain in Scotland.

The study also linked asylum seeker issues to the Fresh Talent initiative (see 'Migrant Workers' section in Chapter 6): 'The single biggest challenge facing Scotland as we move further into the 21st century is our falling population', the former First Minister, Jack McConnell, said, as the country experiences a decrease in the working age population and an increase in the elderly. It appears to be an argument that cuts no ice with the Westminster government, where immigration and asylum are still a reserved matter, despite requests by the Scottish Government that Scotland should operate its own mechanisms for dealing with asylum seekers. So far, the only concession that has been granted is the Immigration Minister's October 2006 allowance for Scotland to process asylum seekers' applications, but he would not rule out dawn raids for the removal of those who fail to have their status legalised.

The methods adopted by the Home Office for the removal of failed asylum seekers caused anger on the part of campaigning groups and distress to the community at large. This came to a head in September 2005 with the forced removal of the Vucaj family, originally from Kosovo. The Children's Commissioner for Scotland, Kathleen Marshall, was fiercely critical and hundreds of people demonstrated outside the immigration offices in Glasgow. When teenage friends of the family from Drumchapel High School became involved, the Scottish Government was obliged to take notice.

The six pupils, four of them children of asylum seekers and two indigenous, gained themselves a headline in *The Herald* – 'Glasgow Girls who Shamed the First Minister into Asylum U-Turn' – when they visited the Scottish Parliament and had an interview with the then First Minister, Jack McConnell (*The Herald*, 24 September 2005). The meeting was the culmination of a six-month campaign by the girls to allow the families of asylum seekers to remain in Scotland.

Rosemary Bennett, Programme Director for Amnesty International, said:

> The Glasgow girls' film painfully demonstrates the effects of government policy on the lives of asylum seekers living in the UK.

Writing in *The Herald* on 25 October 2006, political editor Iain McWhirter argued forcibly that the time had come for Scotland to be making its own decisions about immigration:

> ... the Scottish Government has, for some time, been trying to secure a Scottish 'opt-out' from UK policy, allowing higher points for immigrants wanting to come to Scotland... but so far the Home Office has drawn the line at allowing any significant departure from UK immigration policy, for fear that immigrants would enter the UK by Scotland and immediately move south.

A major frustration in all of this is that most of Glasgow's asylum seekers, given the opportunity, would want to settle here and contribute their skills and talents to the community; people like Ahlam Souidi, who waits every day for the dawn knock that will confirm that her asylum application has finally been refused.

Ahlam Souidi came to Glasgow in 2001, at a time when support mechanisms were few. Forced to leave Algeria because she was a human rights activist, she came with her family to Glasgow, confused and unhappy, and unable to speak a word of English. Housed by the council in the south side of the city, she and her family were racially abused and resented by their neighbours.

Five years on, Ahlam and her family are a credit to the social, cultural and educational support they have received in Glasgow. Her eldest son, a baby when they arrived, is happy at school and her second son, born in the city, is now at nursery. Ahlam's own contributions to the community are remarkable. When Strathclyde Fire Service realised that knowledge of fire safety was lacking in asylum seekers' homes, Ahlam worked with the fire service to produce a visual-only DVD on home and fire safety. The service acknowledged that Ahlam's help in this unique project was crucial.

Ahlam herself, in the film *Asylum Realities*, credits much of her

Village stories.

Kind permission of Liam Stewart.

growth in confidence and pleasure in living in Glasgow to the help she received at the Village Storytelling Centre, a community group based in St James Church, in the Pollok area of the city. The group, through the mechanism of the Village Creative Writing Class, produced *Village Stories*, an anthology of stories and experiences of people from origins as diverse as Iran, Congo and Scotland. The group has also produced *Buffalo Horns*, a collection of experiences, and with their director, Liam Stewart, staged a play called *The Flats*, in which Ahlam Souidi took a principal part, alongside other asylum seekers and people from the local community.

The flats.
Kind permission of Liam Stewart.

In October 2006 Ahlam also took a vocal part in the demonstrations in Glasgow on Global Migrants' Day, and asks to be allowed to live peacefully in the city with her husband and Glaswegian children. After five years, all of Ahlam's appeals have so far been refused.

The work of the Village Storytelling Centre is ongoing, and in 2007 included the Doors Open Project. This project brought together indigenous adults and children in a series of interviews about the asylum seeker experience and those of the Glaswegians. The resulting book is entitled *From Plantation to Pollok, From Kabul to Kennishead*, and there is a website about the project (www.doorsopen.org.uk), which provides a summary of the book and useful background information. The entire project was jointly sponsored by the Heritage LotteryFund, Integration Resources and Glasgow City Council.

The film *Asylum Realities* focused on another asylum seeker family in Glasgow and took views from some of the people who worked with them. Lakhmal Karawela and his wife and children live in Kingsway Court in the Scotstoun area of the city. A Sri Lankan, formerly owner of a thriving business with many employees, Lakhmal's difficulties in his own country arose from his political affiliations. In Glasgow, having joined the Kingsway Court Health and Well-Being partnership, Lakhmal became treasurer to the board of management. Since he is not allowed to take paid employment, this is how he chooses to repay the country that has given him sanctuary.

Frank McAllister, a voluntary worker, and Winnie Watt, Chair of the management committee at Kingsway, spoke on film about the invaluable contribution to local life made by asylum seekers like Lakhmal. The film also featured the International Festival at Kingsway Court, a celebration of cooperation and the multicultural community.

Lakhmal Karawela, who had also been five years in Glasgow when the film was made, also waits for the dreaded dawn knock that will tell him his appeal has been refused.

The controversial practices of the Home Office in detaining failed asylum seekers continued to meet vociferous criticism throughout 2006 when it became apparent in September of that year that the reforms tentatively agreed with the Scottish Government had not been implemented. In that month, two Glasgow families were subjected to the dawn raids: one, an Algerian woman and her two children, aged 11 and two, were taken into custody after immigration officials broke down their door at 6.45 am. Their father had escaped by jumping out of a window.

In a statement released by Glasgow City Council, the headteacher of St Brendan's Primary School said:

> The removal of asylum-seeker children in this way is not only traumatic for them, but is also extremely distressing for the rest of the school community
>
> *The Herald*, 28 September 2006

The strength of feeling about the treatment of asylum seekers in Glasgow was clearly shown on 7 October 2006, when officials were forced to abandon a dawn raid when activists and local people mounted a demonstration outside the home of the family concerned.

Disquiet about such handling of asylum issues has been evident since 2003, when the Scottish Trades Union Council called for a protest at Dungavel Detention Centre in Lanarkshire. The protest called for the closure of this prison-like institution for failed asylum seekers, and demanded that the authorities treat people with respect. People came from all parts of the country to join the demonstration and to festoon the gates and fences with posters and banners. This protest, and others since, have been organised by the Glasgow Campaign to Welcome Refugees.

In 2006 Dungavel was still operating, and while the authorities argue that detention is not prison, it is a fact that the occupants are only allowed limited periods of time outside the buildings.

A dramatic perspective on Dungavel is the play *Petrified Paradise,* a performance event responding to the stories of people who are directly affected by the current asylum and detention system. Catrin Evans, the producer of the play, has said that the performance and discussion aims to 'raise awareness and understanding of the issues that face asylum seekers, their friends, colleagues and neighbours'. The play was a sell-out at the Arches Theatre in Glasgow and in several community venues, and was well received by the critics: 'The physical look and feel of this show is unforgettable, as is the passion with which it is delivered' (Joyce MacMillan, *The Scotsman*).

In March 2006, the Scottish Refugee Council funded a report from the Glasgow Centre for the Child and Society, the aim of which was to explore the experiences of unaccompanied asylum-seeking children and to assess how their needs were being met. These were children who had undergone traumatic experiences in their home country, and who had been brought here by agents; children who had little knowledge of where they were being taken and, for the most part, knew nothing of Scotland. There was no indication given to the researchers that the children had been trafficked. The children experienced stress and anxiety besides the emotional and psychological effects of separation from family and friends in their own countries. One crucial finding, however, was that the children felt safe once they were settled in Scotland.

The Scottish Refugee Council (SRC) and the Big Step, a Glasgow City Council project that supports young people in care, have produced a welcome pack, which includes guidelines for children who arrive in Scotland on their own. The guide aims to explain the asylum system in simple language and inform children of their rights, and about life in this country. The SRC's website suggested that there were around 200 such young people in Scotland in November 2006, and they hoped that the guide would provide some support for them during what is always a difficult time.

The SRC itself is an independent charity dedicated to giving advice, information and assistance to asylum seekers and refugees. It provides specialist services in areas such as housing, welfare, education and employment. The SRC also plays a leading role in policy development and campaigns on refugee issues to ensure that Scotland plays its full part in meeting its legal and humanitarian obligations under the 1951 Convention.

Petrified Paradise.
Kind permission of Liam Stewart.

The work of the SRC is extensive. It provides a family reunion service: people who have been forced to flee their own countries in fear of their lives can become separated from children, husbands or wives, and the service works with agencies such as the Red Cross or the United Nations High Commissioner for Refugees (UNHCR) to organise legal travel for family members to the United Kingdom, and to be reunited. The SRC also runs a free advice line, and other recreational activities such as the Women's Group, which meets in the centre of Glasgow every week. Together with UNHCR, the Refugee Council has launched a research project that supports academics conducting Scottish-based research into asylum and refugee issues.

In the film *Asylum Realities*, the SRC worker Joe Brady clearly demonstrates the value of the Refugee Council when he speaks of operating an emergency rescue service for destitute asylum seekers who literally turn up on the doorstep of the council's Glasgow office. Like Isabelle Ross, who teaches English to asylum seekers in Cardonald College, they hear stories of 'horrific traumas' that have blighted the lives of those who access their service.

Citizens Advice Scotland also plays an important role in the security of asylum seekers in Glasgow, in recent times offering not only advice but training asylum seekers like Ahlam Souidi to become voluntary advisors, so that they can use the experiences gained here to help other asylum seekers. Tim Cowan of the Citizens Advice Bureau in Maryhill feels that the services are more needed than ever, since the asylum system in the United Kingdom has 'lost compassion'.

Winnie Watt of Kingsway Court would agree with him. She describes the asylum seekers she knows of 'living on a knife edge' and calls the methods of forced deportation 'inhuman'. She argues that the authorities seem to have lost sight of the fact that they are dealing with human beings. Recent events might be seen to confirm her views.

With as many as 1,000 families in Glasgow facing removal, the protests from their supporters are growing more vociferous; from the asylum seekers who joined the demonstration at Holyrood in October 2006 to *The Herald* leader writer, who feels that the Home Office decision to transfer the administration of asylum cases to Scotland may be a 'poisoned chalice'.

The newspaper calls for Britain's asylum policy to be 'robust and compassionate' and points out that 70 per cent of asylum appeals are refused, despite complaints from Amnesty International and the

Medical Foundation for the Care of Victims of Torture (*The Herald*, 27 October 2006).

The new approach, when applied in Scotland, is intended to address these issues, by having one official at local level responsible for taking each case forward. This will no doubt help to humanise the bureaucracy, but it is unlikely that it will resolve the situation where the re-settlement package of £3,000 is offered to failed asylum seekers who would rather die than return to the persecution they escaped.

The New Asylum Model (NAM) came into effect in Scotland in March 2007, with a remit to process asylum cases in a matter of weeks rather than months. While ultimately it may be fairer, it will not help those who have waited more than five years for a decision, and *The Herald* calls for an amnesty for these people on both 'pragmatic and humanitarian' grounds. For people like Ahlam Souidi, who voices the pleas of many in her position when she says, 'I can never go back'.

The solution to the failed asylum seekers who do not return to their home countries that has been implemented by the Home Office, is to withdraw all benefits. At the beginning of November 2006, Amnesty International claimed that failed asylum seekers were becoming destitute when their home country refused to take them back. The report spoke of the 'inhuman and ineffective policy' of denying support to failed asylum seekers. Further condemnation of this policy was demonstrated in an open letter in *The Herald*, signed by a long list of organisations and campaigners dedicated to the welfare of asylum seekers:

> We are supporting a wide campaign calling on the UK government to ensure that rejected asylum seekers unable to return home are granted the right to remain in the UK and live secure and dignified lives
>
> *The Herald*, 7 November 2006

Throughout Glasgow's history of migrants and immigrants, who were not always welcomed, ultimately the city has absorbed and assimilated the incomers until they become, by their own choice, wholly Glaswegian.

Mohsen Saad, a Somalian and the third story in *Asylum Realities*, was only 16 years old when he arrived in Glasgow seeking asylum. He had no friends here and only a basic grasp of English. Mohsen was fortunate in that he was granted asylum within eight months, and from then his life developed in a positive way, subsequently studying drama at Langside

College. 'The Scottish Refugee Council took very good care of me', Mohsen says. 'They did everything for me. It has been an adventure. Glasgow made me who I am' (*The Herald*, 24 October 2006).

Now aged 20, Mohsen and a friend from Congo founded Fugees United in 2005, a collection of young African musicians with something to say about their world. In June 2007 a book about the wider experience of refugees was launched in Glasgow by Counterpoint, an arm of the British Council. The book, *From Outside In – Refugees and British Society*, is a collection of fiction, memoirs and poetry exploring the British experience of the newly arrived. The new Home Office procedures for the fast-tracking of asylum applications has resulted in what have been termed 'legacy cases' – those whose asylum requests have languished for a number of years, and it is the intention to have all of these cases resolved by 2011.

Meanwhile, distressing experiences continue to be reported in the press, such as that of a Pakistani woman: 'The future remains uncertain for single mother Misbah Ali, her six-year old son Sharhoiz and daughter Noor', taken to London for deportation but winning a 'last-gasp' reprieve and gladly returning to their home in Glasgow (Wendy Miller, *The Herald*, 10 August 2007). Elsewhere in the same paper, a correspondent commented that 'asylum policy is the moral test of a nation' (8 August 2007). To date, control over that policy remains a reserved matter for the Westminster Parliament.

In Scottish terms, the asylum story in 2007 gives some positive indications for the future. The new Scottish Nationalist Party administration in Holyrood continues the policy of opposition to forced removals, particularly when children are involved, and draws attention to the terms of the UNESCO policy on the 'Rights of the Child', which stresses that an asylum-seeker child has exactly the same rights as any other child. To this end, asylum-seeker children of three and four years of age are to be given nursery places, while, at the other end of the spectrum, suitably qualified young people will be eligible to apply for university entrance on the same basis as other Scottish school leavers. This move has been brought about by the dedicated lobbying of Universities Scotland, representative of university principals, and the Scottish Refugee Council. Fiona Hyslop, Education Secretary, has rejected the criticism that giving Scottish university places to asylum seekers would create a 'magnet' for others seeking to come to the United Kingdom. She has argued that these are the children of well-established families, and that the current practice of the Home Office in dealing with new cases within six months would ensure that this would not happen. In 2007–2008 not more than 18 young people from asylum-seeker families are likely to apply for such places.

Another hopeful note for asylum seekers who find themselves in Glasgow was struck by the publication of a report by the Commission for Racial Equality. 'There is received wisdom that Scotland tends to be more welcoming because of a strong sense of national identity' (Commission for Racial Equality Report, March 2007). The report goes on to suggest that such a powerful sense of identity lessens the perception of threat to the indigenous population by new arrivals. It is encouraging for Glaswegians that this might be the case; however, it would be a disservice to the experience of asylum seekers and refugees in Glasgow to suggest that this renders them immune to harassment and abuse in their daily lives. It may simply be less than elsewhere in the United Kingdom. Irene Graham, formerly Glasgow's spokeswoman on equality issues, said that 'Glasgow has a proud history of giving refuge to those who are fleeing persecution', and while this is borne out in the earlier chapters of this book, it almost goes without saying that this city, its council and many Glaswegians of good will, continually strive to keep that proud history alive. But it is a sad fact that some of the asylum seekers mentioned above and many more, acknowledged if not named, may have been removed from Glasgow by the time these words are read.

CHAPTER 10

The Changing Scene, 2016

IN 2006, Tim Cowan of the Citizens Advice Bureau in Maryhill, Glasgow, expressed the view that the asylum system in the UK had 'lost compassion.' The CAB is only one of many non-governmental agencies who reach out to individuals who often have harrowing tales to tell of their journeys to Scotland and safety. Prominent amongst these is the Scottish Refugee Council, the Convention of Scottish Local Authorities (COSLA) via the Scotland Strategic Migration Partnership, Glasgow Caring City, Migrant Help UK, the Refugee Survival Trust and many community-run organisations and individuals who take on this role in a voluntary capacity. In addition, The Commission for Racial Equality, Scotland, set up to implement the Race Relations Act 1976, has now been absorbed into the Equality and Human Rights Commission.

All of these organs work to help seekers of asylum and refugees, but disturbingly, now in 2016, ten years after Tim Cowan's lament, there are still many stories of unfeeling bureaucracy and iron-clad regulations leading to destitution and deportation. Migrant Help in particular, who launched their asylum programme in 2014, has helped 40,000 clients in the less than two years from its founding. It is partnered with the Home Office in an effort to design a more efficient model of support for those who are often left to navigate complex bureaucracy. It is, however, this same Home Office which is frequently the source of much distress in the migrant experience. For example, in February 2016, the Scottish Refugee Council called for an independent inquiry into 'dehumanising treatment' by the private company contracted to provide accommodation for asylum seekers in Glasgow. The Home Office outsources these in Glasgow to SERCO, provider of multi-national services, whose personnel were reported to treat asylum seekers in 'disgraceful' ways. (*The Times*, February 2016)

How these aspects of life for immigrants, asylum seekers or refugees will change following the most recent Immigration Act, which received its Royal Assent on 12 May 2016, remains to be seen. The Act, in summary sets out:

to make provision about the law on immigration and asylum; to make provision about access to services, facilities, licences and work by reference to immigration status; to make provision about the Director of Labour Market Enforcement; to make provision about language requirements for public sector workers; to make provision about fees for passports and civil registration; and for connected purposes.

In 2014 Prime Minister David Cameron sought to have some features of EU migration law watered down in the face of increasing numbers coming from the other 27 other countries of the European Union, as they are entitled to do. Britain is not part of the Schengen agreement of 1985, which came in to effect in 1995. Schengen allows travel without passports in all countries of the EU, and while the UK is obliged to allow free movement of labour, border controls remain. Moreover, the current volume of refugee movements and increasing incidence of terrorism is causing European governments to question Schengen. It was reportedly 'hanging in the balance' (www.independent.co.uk. January 2016).

The British concessions re EU migration achieved by the Prime Minister included:

Work-based benefits 'phased in over a four year period', and if there are 'exceptional' levels of migration the UK will operate an 'emergency brake' for seven years.

Child benefit for the children of migrants living overseas will be paid at a rate consistent with the cost of living in their home countries; applicable immediately for new arrivals and from 2020 for existing claimants.

In due course EU Treaties will be amended to state explicitly that references to the requirement to 'seek ever closer union' between Member States 'do not apply to the United Kingdom.'

These conditions and others are predominantly a feature of the unease seen in parts of the UK about increasing levels of migration from a European Union suspected to grow even larger and closer in coming decades, and may well inform the outcome of the EU Referendum on Thursday, 23 June 2016. It is an emotive and controversial subject. While critics worry about the pressure on schools, hospitals or the health service from too many migrants, the other side of the argument claims that the UK needs the migrants since agriculture, the NHS, tourism and some manufacturing cannot function without them. It is a fact that one in every five care workers in Britain is an immigrant. Besides, it is also the case that EU migrants contribute more in tax than they draw in benefit. In 2013/14 EU workers paid £2.5 billion in taxes. Currently there are three million EU migrants living in Britain and over two million Britons living in Europe. The eligible public of the entire British Isles, plus Gibraltar, will vote on whether to remain part of the European Union or leave. This will be the first time the question has been asked since 1975. Regardless of the result of this vote, which might change the landscape of migration from Europe, immigration from other parts of the world will remain, particularly for asylum seekers and refugees.

Undoubtedly, in 2016, immigration is a particularly difficult subject for governments throughout Europe and beyond, since we are confronting the greatest movement of people fleeing for their lives from war-torn Syria and from other states in the Middle East since immediately after the Second World War. The number of adults and children who have given their lives to the Mediterranean Sea at the hands of criminal traffickers has risen to thousands in recent times (A UN figure put deaths in this year alone at more than 2,500). By 2015 almost one million people had passed through Greece seeking asylum. European governments face serious practical and moral issues regarding the settlement of these enormous numbers of displaced and dispossessed peoples. On 4 September 2015, a small Syrian boy, Alan Kurdi, was found dead, washed up on a beach in Turkey. The tragedy of this three year old provoked emotional responses around the world, and people flocked to supply aid of every description for the survivors, but by mid-2016 no viable solution to this refugee crisis has been promulgated by the European Union.

In September 2014 Scottish voters went to the polls to decide whether Scotland should remain part of the United Kingdom, or leave. In an unprecedented turn-out the No vote won by 55 per cent as against 45 per cent for Yes. Subsequently the UK government set up the Smith Commission, to examine the ways in which more powers could be devolved to Scotland. In the General Election which followed, the Scottish National Party sent 56 MPs to Westminster and in the Scottish Election of May 2016, 63 Scottish National MSPs took their seats in the Holyrood Parliament in Edinburgh in addition to six independence supporting members of the Green Party. In 2016 the Scotland Act set out the reforms agreed for Scotland: to be in control of aspects of taxation, certain welfare benefits, employment law and a long list of other competencies including

Equal Opportunities. (www. legislation. gov.uk) It did not, however, devolve immigration law, which remains in sole control of the Westminster Government.

The latest migration figures (Office of National Statistics Quarterly Report, February 2016) show that in the year to September 2015, the estimated number of EU citizens coming to the UK as a whole was 257,000. Of those, 165,000 came for work-related reasons, 96,000 for a definite job and 69,000 seeking employment. In addition, at the end of 2015 there were almost 40,000 asylum seekers in the UK from outwith the EU.

The largest number of applications for asylum came from Eritrea, closely followed by Iran, Pakistan, Sudan and almost 3,000 from Syria. In September 2015 the Prime Minister announced the extension of the Syrian Vulnerable Persons Resettlement Scheme to allow the resettlement of up to 20,000 Syrian refugees over the subsequent five years. Meantime in 2015, 1,337 Syrians were identified as in need of protection. In 2015 the number of refugees from all destinations granted permission to remain permanently in Britain was under 90,000, considerably fewer than in the previous five years.

An aspect of the figures which must be taken into account is the fact that at any time considerable numbers emigrate from the UK – for work, going home, or affected by the economic downturn. In Scotland's case, the figures for between mid 2014 and 2015 show that net migration stood at 19,600. While 37,800 people arrived, 18,200 left.

In Glasgow, the latest Census in 2011, showed that the city had a population of just under 600,000. In terms of black and ethnic minority communities the largest Scottish cities had the highest percentages – Glasgow City 12 per cent, City of Edinburgh and Aberdeen 8 per cent and Dundee 6 per cent. For Scotland as a whole, some 369,000 or 7 per cent of the population have been born outside the UK: furthermore 55 per cent of those born outside the UK arrived here between 2004 and 2011. As a matter of interest, in Glasgow, those who described themselves as Black, African and Caribbean rose from 1,792 in the 2001 Census to 14,246 in 2011. The Pakistani population was 22,405, Indian 8,640, and Bangladeshi 458. There are also 3,000 people of Roma origin in Scotland.

Recently marking the UN Day for the Elimination of Racial Discrimination, the Scottish Parliament endorsed the Equality and Human Rights Commission. The government has renewed its approach to race equality, working in partnership with a range of organisations. A new Race Equality Framework for Scotland, 2016–2030, was launched in March 2016. The

Scottish Government took the lead in this, with input from key stake-holders and independent support from CRER, the Coalition for Racial Equality and Rights. The key components included a Community Ambassadors Programme to ensure widespread consultation with black and ethnic minority communities across Scotland. It should be noted that while significant effort is being expended to make this country a safe and secure home for any individual in the groups discussed in this book, social media has become a new and distressing source of racial harassment, particularly for vulnerable young people.

The Scottish Government, as it stands in 2016, has a quite different perspective on immigration from that of Westminster, but does not have the power to put this into practice. The post-study work visa, intro-duced by the UK government in 2002, allowed students from outwith the EU to remain in the country for at least two years after graduating from a Higher Education institution. Scotland, particularly the Highlands, does not have a problem of overpopulation therefore for some of these able people to remain, to work and settle in the country, was welcomed by the Scottish Government. However, the UK government scrapped the scheme in 2012, claiming abuse. All five political parties in Holyrood have since backed the re-introduction of the visas in Scotland. The cross party group made ten recommendations, covering who should qualify and the conditions which should be met. The Scottish report out-lined, 'A clear and practical path to allow talented graduates to remain in Scotland.' The Home Office has no plans to change the system.

A number of people have been caught in the trap of this retrospective legislation, none more so than the Brain family. Gregg and Kathryn Brain left their home in Australia and came to Scotland with their infant son Lachlan in 2010, to live in Dingwall; made welcome as contributing to the re-population of the Highlands. Kathryn studied for a degree and Lachlan was enrolled in a Gaelic medium primary school. Five years later, although Gregg and Kathryn had offers of jobs and Lachlan was a fluent Gaelic speaker, they encountered the intransigence of the Home Office and had to leave the UK. Considerable anger was generated in the press regarding the Brain family, with the instant communication of the present day ensuring that the story became global. Support came from all quarters, including the Gaelic League of New York. They were due to leave Scotland in August 2016.

The Brains should have been welcome immigrants in Scotland.

Political commentator Carolyn Leckie has written in *The National* newspaper about others who were in a similar plight and were often to be returned to doubtful destinations. In 2014 almost 39,000 people were deported from Britain – there is no separate figure for Scotland. People like Min Lin, with her five year old daughter and baby son, deported to China in a dawn raid in November 2015. Or Beverely Kainjii, settled in Glasgow before deportation to Namibia.

But perhaps the most incomprehensible story of all was that of Olivier Mondeke Monongo. Olivier had been in Scotland since 2002, planning to spend the rest of his life here with his five children, who were born in Glasgow. As a Congolese asylum seeker he was finally granted temporary leave to remain in 2010. The condition was lifted in 2013, and Olivier began to study for his 'Life in the UK' test, a crucial element of British citizenship. Olivier had worked steadily in a voluntary capacity as an assistant mental health nurse, a minister and court interpreter. He was trusted by the NHS to provide interpreters for vulnerable patients, and by Glasgow Sheriff Court. Olivier passed the test but was not allowed to call himself Scottish. His unpaid role with the Red Cross charity's tracing service helped to put asylum seekers in touch with families in their home countries. Immigration officials rejected his application for citizenship based on this voluntary work. The 'good character' rules prohibit unpaid work by asylum seekers or refugees. Olivier Mondeke Monongo failed the character test.

Others who fall foul of inefficient or careless bureaucracy find themselves glad of the Refugee Survival Trust. This charity based in Edinburgh does exactly what its name suggests – it helps refugees to survive. On its website there is a short film narrated by the writer AL Kennedy, who is telling the stories of a number of individuals literally saved from hunger by the small grants made to them by the trust. Some of these are children, made destitute after winning the right to stay. People seeking sanctuary in UK receive Home Office funding for 28 days, which ends when a final decision is made. Successful claimants go on to welfare benefits; unsuccessful transitions leave people unsupported. The Refugee Survival Trust provided 900 destitution grants between April 2013 – March 2016. At that time they were supporting 200 children. (www.rst.org.uk)

The stories voiced by writer AL Kennedy are of individuals who were in Scotland already, who, as asylum seekers or refugees were logged in the system – like Mariam, from Eritrea, whose village was destroyed and whose family was killed. She was raped. She tried to claim asylum in Glasgow but was unable to because she is single. Single people must go to Croydon, in the south of England. She did not have the bus fare, because she was destitute. Or Yahia, an Iraqi Christian, also seeking asylum in Glasgow. His wife was killed, his life threatened and he came to Glasgow with his young son. His asylum funding was cancelled by mistake and agents bringing him emergency tokens were foiled by his broken doorbell, and left.

AL Kennedy gives details of several more desperate cases: people who became the victims of harsh rules or mistakes by the bureaucracy through no fault of their own. Scotland is committed to taking 2,000 of the new Syrian refugees, whose survival might be assured if they arrive in the glare of publicity generated by the tragedies of their friends, neighbours or relatives. The First Minister of Scotland, Nicola Sturgeon said, 'Scotland is ready and willing to do all that we can to help refugees.'

Newspaper reports to date suggest that the Syrian refugees already in Scotland feel welcome. A 'cup of kindness' football tournament in North Lanarkshire had ten refugees and staff from the re-settlement programme take part. Twelve refugee families arrived in Scotland in 2015 to live in Coatbridge and Airdrie. Other families have been located on the Isle of Bute. Mansour Zalaf said, 'We were in Syria during the war. It was a terrible life, being under the torture and detention of the regime.' While asylum seekers, refugees and other migrants may occasionally suffer at the hands of inefficient administration, no person will be tortured in any part of the United Kingdom. Detention however, remains an unfortunate part of the programme for some.

In March 2015, MSP Liam Brady publicised the fact that failed asylum seekers were still being detained, some for more than one year at a time, and that amongst those were children. Following that, in March 2016 the BBC claimed that there were still 185 detainees in Dungavel in Scotland, two of whom had been held for more than a year. The UK is the only country in the EU which has no cap on how long people can be detained. In the event of Scotland becoming an independent nation, The Scottish National Party, if in power, would close Dungavel.

Hope for some women, however, can reside in Saheliya, a charitable and voluntary organisation based in Edinburgh. In 2016 Saheliya won the Scottish Council for Voluntary Organisations (SCVO) charity award for their work. In 1992 the organisation was set up to provide a mental wellbeing service for black and ethnic minority women. In the year to June 2016, their 33 multi-lingual staff, who speak 28 languages, worked

with no less than 986 women, including asylum seekers and refugees from 39 countries. (www.saheliya.co.uk)

Meantime, Refugee Festival Week took place between 14 June – 26 June 2016. It is an annual festival, coordinated by the Scottish Refugee Council, presenting a whole range of activities from art projects, drama, talks, films and exhibitions in venues around the country, raising the profile and telling the stories, good and bad, of the refugee experience before and after finding sanctuary in Scotland.

Finally, on 17 June 2016, Medecins Sans Frontieres, the globally respected charity, announced that it would no longer accept funding from the European Union in the light of the community's 'shameful response' to the refugee crisis. The EU's policy of 'damaging deterrence' and its increasing attempts to 'push people and their suffering away from European shores' has brought the charity to a point where it will forego £50 million pounds of funding rather than accept the community's actions. The charity is incensed by the EU Turkey deportation agreement which has left thousands trapped in squalid camps in Greece. It is also furious at the EU's plans to reward African dictators who prevent people fleeing their countries.

Postscript: July 2016

The above-mentioned referendum on membership of the European Union took place on 23 June. The question asked was:

'Should the United Kingdom remain a member of the European Union, or leave the European Union?'

The national result was – Turn-out 72.2%, of which 16,141,241 registered voters chose to Remain (48.1%) and 17,410,742. voted to Leave (51.9%.) of a total electorate of 46,500,001.

This breaks down by country to:

England	Remain 46.8%	Leave 53.2%
Wales	Remain 48.3%	Leave 51.7%
Northern Ireland	Remain 55.7%	Leave 44.3%
Scotland	Remain 62%	Leave 38%

(electoralcommission.org.uk)

On 24 June the UK and the EU, awoke to the fact that a majority of the British public had voted to leave the European Union. Later that morning the Prime Minister David Cameron announced his resignation.

A glance at the figures demonstrates that the choices made were not uniform across the four countries which make up the United Kingdom, and much of the subsequent publicity revealed that immigration had indeed served to inform the decision of many Leave voters. These results were followed by incidents of xenophobia and racism towards minorities from the EU and elsewhere. In Scotland, however, the police reported that there had been no appreciable rise in incidents since 24 June.

Police Scotland's Barry McEwan said there had been no corresponding rise in hate crimes in Scotland: 'At this time we have not witnessed any increase in the level of reports being received.' (*The National*, 1 July 2016)

In Holyrood, First Minister of Scotland Nicola Sturgeon, with the support of all parties in the Scottish Government, made it clear, in the post-referendum climate, that migrants, immigrants, refugees or asylum seekers will continue to find an official welcome in Scotland. Thus it is to be wished that, like the Jewish, Irish, Italian or later incomers whose stories are told above, those whose journeys end in Glasgow or other parts of Scotland, will ultimately come to feel that 'they belong'.

Bibliography

Archives

Colquoun, William. Letters 1770–1775 (SRA)
Cunningham, J. Letter Book (SRA)
Police Register 1850–1900 (SRA)
Poor Law Applications (Irish Series, Glasgow 1858) (SRA)

British Immigration Legislation in the 20th Century

1905	Aliens Act
1914–19	Aliens Restriction Acts
1914	Imperial Act
1947	Polish Resettlement Act
1948	British Nationality Act
1962	Commonwealth Immigrant Act
1968	Commonwealth Immigrant Act
1971	Immigration Act
1981	British Nationality Act
1983	British Nationality Act (+ Amendments)

Books

Bolitho, W. *Cancer of Empire* (Putnam's Sons Ltd., Glasgow 1924)

Book of Remembrance (Glasgow Corporation 1902)

Bowers, C. and File, N. *Black Settlers in Britain* (Heinemann, London 1980)

Brennan, T. *Reshaping of a City* (House of Grant, Glasgow 1959)

British Jewry Book of Honour (Caxton Publishing, London 1919)

Brogan, C. *The Glasgow Story* (Muller, London 1952)

Cleland, J. *Tracts* (Glasgow 1837)

Collins, K. (ed.) *Aspects of Scottish Jewry* (Glasgow Jewish Representative Council 1987)

Collins, K. *Second City Jewry – The Jews of Glasgow in the Age of Expansion 1790–1919* (Scottish Jewish Archives Centre 1990)

Cowan, E. *Spring Remembered* (Southside, Edinburgh 1974)

Cunnison and Gilfillan. *Third Statistical Account of Scotland* (Glasgow 1957)

Daiches, D. *Glasgow* (Deutsch, London 1977)

Desai, R. *Indian Immigrants in Britain* (Oxford University Press, London 1963)

Eyre Todd, G. *History of Glasgow* (Glasgow 1934)

Freedman, M. *A Minority in Britain* (Valentine Mitchell, London 1955)

Fryer, P. *Staying Power: A History of Black People in Britain* (Pluto Press, London 1984)

Fullarton and Baird. *Remarks on Evils Affecting the Highlands and Islands* (Glasgow 1838)

Grant, I. F. *Highland Folk Ways* (Routledge & Kegan Paul, London 1961)

Hammerton, J. A. *Sketches from Glasgow* (Glasgow 1893)

Handley, J. *The Irish in Scotland* (Cork University Press, Cork 1943)

Henderson, I. *Scotland, Kirk and People* (Clark, Edinburgh 1969)

Hiro, D. *Black British: White British* (Eyre & Spottiswode, London 1971)

House, J. *The Heart of Glasgow* (Hutchison, Glasgow 1972)

Husband, C. (ed.) *Race in Britain Today* (Hutchison, London 1982)

Huxley, E. *Back Streets: New World* (Chatto & Windus, London 1964)

Kaplan H. and Hutt, C. (eds) *A Scottish Shtetl: Jewish Life in the Gorbals 1880–1974* (Glasgow 1984)

Kiernan, V. G. *Lords of Human Kind* (Baylis & Son, London 1969)

Levy, A. *Origins of Glasgow Jewry* (Jewish Historical Society, Glasgow 1956)

McGregor, G. *History of Glasgow* (Morison, Glasgow 1981)

McKenzie, A. *History of Highland Clearances* (Inverness 1883)

McKinnon, K. *Phoenix Bird Takeaway* (A & C Black, London 1973)

McUre, H. *History of Glasgow* (Duncan, Glasgow 1736)

Majundar and Copra. *Main Currents of Indian History* (Sterling, New Delhi 1979)

New Cambridge Modern History Vol. III

Nichol, H. *Glasgow and the Tobacco Lords* (Longman, London 1966)

O'Brien, C. C. and O'Brien, M. A. *A Concise History of Ireland* (Thames & Hudson, London 1972)

Odyssey Transcripts BBC (Polygon Books, Edinburgh)

Pagan (ed.) *Past and Present* Vols. 1–111 (Glasgow 1886)

Parkes, J. *A History of the Jewish People* (Weidenfeld & Nicolson 1962)

Patterns of Racism (Institute of Race Relations, London 1982)

Phillips, A. *Origins of the First Jewish Community in Scotland* (Donald, Edinburgh 1973)

Roots of Racism (Institute of Race Relations, London 1982)

Rose, E. B. *Colour and Citizenship* (Oxford University Press, London 1969)

Runnymede Trust *Britain's Black Population* (Heinemann, London 1980)

Smout, T. C. *A History of the Scottish People* (Collins, Glasgow 1969)

Walvin, J. *Passage to Britain* (Penguin, London 1984)

Watson, J. L. *Between Two Cultures* (Blackwell, London 1971)

Working Together (Scottish International Labour Council, Glasgow)

Newspapers, Articles, Pamphlets and Reports

The Bailie Vols. 35–36 (Glasgow 1889–90)

A Brief View of Negro Slavery, 1823 (SRA)

An Lochran, Gaelic Arts Strategy Doc., 2006

Census (Scotland) 1851

Census (Scotland) 2001

Children's Employment Commission (Scotland): First Report 1863

Chinese Community in Strathclyde: Extract from Report of House of Commons Race Relations Committee 14th May 1984

Chinese Community News – Chinese Community Development Partnership 2006

City of Glasgow; A Study of the Diet of the Labouring Classes 1911–1912 (SRA)

Collier, A. 'Polish Community Welcomes the Pope' *Scottish Field*, May 1982

Colpi, T. 'The Italian Migration to Scotland: Fact, Fiction and the Future'. In Dutto, M. (ed.) *The Italians in Scotland: Their Language and Culture*. Edinburgh University Press, 1986 Community Voice, CRC. June, 1985

Davies, N. 'Poland's Dream of Past Glory'. *History Today*, November 1982

Daily Record – August 2006, September 2006

Education for All, Swann Committee, HMSO. April 1985

Education of Ethnic Minorities in Strathclyde. HMI Report, SED 1983

Edwards, P. 'History of the Blacks in Britain', *History Today*, September 1981

Emigration (Scotland): Select Committee: First Report 1841.

Fowler, B. Littlewood, B. and Madigan, R. 'Sorry the Job has been taken'. *New Society*, April 1977

Glasgow Chamber of Commerce Journal 1974–5

Glasgow Chinese Women's Group Report – 1997

Glasgow Corporation Transport Dept. Minutes 1950–60

Glasgow Evening Citizen March 1894 – June 1943

Glasgow Evening Times September 1980 – July 1983

Glasgow Evening Times – March 2005, July 2005

Glasgow Herald July 1842, January 1892, April 1892, October 1913, August 1938, December 1938, September 1942, September 1973, December 1984, June 1985

The Herald – September 2005, Sepembert 2006, October 2006, November 2006, August 2007

Howard, M. 'Empire, Race and War in pre. 19th Century Britain', *History Today*, December 1981

Jackson, B. and Garvey, A. 'Chinese Children in Britain', *New Society*, October 1974

Jewish Chronicle, 1911

Jewish Echo, 1928, 1939

Journal of the Statistical Society Vol. 24 1861

Kearsley, G. W. and Scrivastava, S. R. 'Spatial Evolution of Glasgow's Asian Community', *Scottish Geographical*, September 1974

Koczy, L. *Scottish-Polish Society Historical Review* 1980

Kut-O Buddhist Association. Report 2003

Leslie, R. F. Polish Question, *Historical Review* Pamphlet 1964

Liam Stewart (ed.) Village Stories. (Village Storyelling Centre 2005)

McKenzie, A. *Trial of Patrick Sellar*, Inverness 1883.

Mackenzie, D. 'The Incomers', *Scotland*, November 1964.

Maan, B. *Gorbals View* (Indian and Pakistani Column) 1967

Marshall, P. J. 'European Imperialism in the 19th Century' *History Today*, May 1982

Miller, H. Police Return: 1038, Destitute Persons in Glasgow, 1841

The National, June 2016

Odyssey Transcripts. BBC Edinburgh, Polygon Books

Poet's Box (Poems, Songs, Sketches) (ML)

Polish Exile, Edinburgh 1833

Ross, W. A. 'Highland Emigration', *Scottish Geographical*, May 1934

Royal Commission of Poorer Classes in Ireland. 1st Report 1835. Appendix G: Report on the State of the Irish Poor in Great Britain 1835. Vols. 30–34

Church of Scotland. General Assembly Report: The Menace of the Irish Race to our Scottish Nationality. Edinburgh 1923

Scotland on Sunday – September 2006, October 2006

La Scozia, 1908

Stow College Glasgow Chinese School Pamphlet – 2000

Sunday Herald – August 2007

The Scots-Italians, Mercator Press, 2006

'The Silent Minority. The Chinese in Britain'. Report of the Fourth National Congress. Commonwealth Institute 1982 Sunday Trading (Glasgow): House of Commons Select Committee Report. 1906

Tindall, G. 'Bombay, City of Gold'. *History Today*, May 1982

Village Stories – Ed. Liam Stewart – Village Storytelling Centre 2005

Walvin, J. 'The 18th Century'. *History Today*, September 1982

Wing Ho Chinese Elderly Centre Report – 2005

DVDs

Asylum Realities (Scottish Refugee Council 2006)

Online Resources and Websites

BBC News   www.bbcnews.co.uk
Daily Record   ww.dailyrecord.org.uk
The Herald   www.theherald.co.uk
Scotsman Newpapers   www.scotsman.com
Sunday Herald   www.sundayherald.com
Newsquest Online Archives   www.newsquest.co.uk
Jewish Telegraph   www.jewish telegraph.com
iwitness   www.iwitness.co.uk

African and Caribbean
  Network Scotland   www.paperclip.org.uk
Citizens Advice Scotland   www.cas.org.uk
Comhaltas (Irish Arts)   www.comhaltas.com
Comunn na Gaidhlig   www.cnag.org.uk
Convention of Local Authorities   www.cosla.gov.uk
Franchi Finnieston (Solicitors)   www.franchifinnieston.co.uk
Glasgow Anti-Racist Alliance   www.gara.org.uk
Glasgow Centre for the Child Society   www.gccs.gla.ac.uk
Glasgow City Council   www.glasgow.gov.uk
Glasgow City Council Museums   www.glasgowmuseums.com
Glasgow Chinese School   www.glasgowchineseschool.org
Glasgow Irish Minstrels   www.glasgowirishminstrels.co.uk
Glasgow University Muslim Students
  Association   www.gumsa.quantumretrieval.co.uk/site
Hannah Frank   www.hannahfrank.org.uk
Hey Now Radio   www.radioheynow.com
The Home Office   www.ukvisas.gov.uk
The Home Office   www.homeoffice.gov.uk
iwitness   www.iwitness.co.uk
Jewish Telegraph   www.jewish telegraph.com
Labour Party   www.labour.org.ok
Newsquest Online Archives   www.newsquest.co.uk
Office of Public Sector Information   www.opsi.gov.uk/acts1998
Oxfam Scotland   www.oxfam.org.uk/scotland
Polish Taste Delicatessen   www.polishtaste.co.uk
Proiseact nan Ealan

(The Gaelic Arts Agency)	www.gaelic-arts.com (Gaelic site)
Radio Hey Now	www.radioheynow.com
ricefield Chinese Arts	www.ricefield.co.uk
Scotland China Association	www.scotchina.org
Scottish Council Jewish Communities	www.j-scot.org.uk
Scottish Government	www.scotland.gov.uk
Scottish Government	www.scotlandistheplace.co.uk
Scottish Refugee Council	www.scottishrefugeecouncil.org.uk
Scottish Trades Union Council	www.stuc.org.uk
Sikorsli Polish Club Glasgow	www.sikorskipolishclub.org.uk
Tir Connaill Harps (GAC)	www.conaill.fsnet.co.uk
United Nations Refugee Convention (1951)	www.unhchr.ch/html
University of Glasgow	www.gla.ac.uk
University of Strathclyde	www.strath.ac.uk
West Dunbarton Council	www.west-dunbarton.gov.uk
Wikipedia Online Encyclopaedia	www.wikipedia.org

Abbreviations

ML	The Mitchell Library
SRA	Strathclyde Regional Archives

Index

Some other books published by **LUATH** PRESS

Glasgow By the Way, But

John Cairney

ISBN 1-906307-10-5 PBK £7.99

Glasgow to me is the ugly face that launched a thousand quips. If you're born in Glasgow you're born with a sense of humour. It's the only passport you need to get beyond its boundaries. I've gone around the world several times – I don't know if I've held Glasgow in front of me or dragged it behind me – but I've never been far from her in all that time. Glasgow is a working-class city with a heart of gold. It's Scotland's Chicago, with a streak of New York. It may be the ugly sister of Scotland's cities, but it's the one everybody fancies once they get to know her.
JOHN CAIRNEY

Do you love going to the pictures? Live for the season's Old Firm match? Have a 'rerr' singer in the family? Long to dance under the stars in the Barras ballroom? Is your idea of a local hero Lobby Dosser? And who needs Bob Dylan when you have Matt McGinn?

In this collection of personal anecdotes, John Cairney takes you on a tour of *his* Glasgow, introducing the people and places that have shaped it. Full of the humour, tension and patter that characterises Scotland's most charismatic city, everyone will be sure to find a part of their own Glasgow reflected in Cairney's honest evocation of his home city. *Glasgow by the way, but* is the written tribute Glasgow has been waiting for, from one of its most famous sons.

A Glasgow Mosaic
Cultural Icons of the City

Ian R Mitchell

ISBN 978-1-908373-66-3 PBK £9.99

With this book is completed a trilogy of works begun in 2005 with *This City Now: Glasgow and its Working Class Past*, and continuing with *Clydeside; Red Orange and Green* in 2009. The three books have all had similar aims in trying to raise the profile of forgotten or neglected areas and aspects of Glasgow and its history, in a small way trying to boost the esteem in which such places are held by the people who live in there and by those who visit. Moving away slightly from the working class focus, this third instalment presents a broad view of Glasgow's industrial, social and intellectual history.

From public art to socialist memorials, and from factories to cultural hubs, Ian Mitchell takes the reader on a guided tour of Glasgow, outlining walking routes which encompass the city's forgotten icons.

Praise for the Author

Mitchell pulls back the curtain on Clydeside communities, looking beyond the quieted mills and coal mines to provide a rich working class history, too often over-looked and underappreciated.

This Road is Red

Alison Irvine

ISBN 978-1-910021-53-8 PBK £8.99

It is 1964. Red Road is rising out of the fields. To the families who move in, it is a dream and a shining future.

It is 2010. The Red Road Flats are scheduled for demolition. Imhabited only by intrepid asylum seekers and a few stubborn locals, the once vibrant scheme is now tired and out of time.

Between those dates are the people who filled the flats with their laughter, life and drama. Their stories are linked by the buildings; the sway and buffet of the tower blocks in the wind, the creaky lifts, the views and the vertigo.

This Road is Red is a compelling and subtle novel of Glasgow.

This is a spirited, funny and moving novel, and a wonderfully human testament to the community from which it developed.
SALTIRE SOCIETY AWARD JUDGES

Irvine does for Glasgow what Irvine Welsh has done for Edinburgh – imagining a city through its fringes, fearlessly and without frills.
PROFESSOR WILLY MALEY, University of Glasgow

Irvine's stories are by turns sad, frightening, moving, dark, occasionally wickedly funny and always compelling.
MORNING STAR

Walking Through Glasgow's Industrial Past

Ian R Mitchell

ISBN 978-1-910021-15-6 PBK £7.99

Join Ian R Mitchell on a series of walks through Glasgow's industrial past as he retrieves the hidden architectural, cultural and historical riches of some of Glasgow's industrial and working-class districts.

Many who enjoy the fruits of Glasgow's recent gentrification may be surprised and delighted by the gems Ian Mitchell has uncovered beyond the usual haunts.

An enthusiastic walker and knowledgeable historian, he invites us to recapture the social and political history of the working class in Glasgow. Taking in area including Pollokshaws, Springburn, Maryhill

and Parkhead, Mitchell reveals the buildings that go unnoticed every day yet are worthy of so much more attention, and the stories behind them and their inhabitants.

Praise for *This City Now*

A plethora of fascinating historical facts... Mitchell takes us behind [Glasgow's] façade to unveil some real treasures... the warmth and wit of working-class Glasgow provides the book's heart and soul.
DAILY MAIL

Details of these and all other books published by Luath Press can be found at **www.luath.co.uk**

Luath Press Limited

committed to publishing well written books worth reading

LUATH PRESS takes its name from Robert Burns, whose little collie Luath (*Gael.*, swift or nimble) tripped up Jean Armour at a wedding and gave him the chance to speak to the woman who was to be his wife and the abiding love of his life. Burns called one of 'The Twa Dogs' Luath after Cuchullin's hunting dog in Ossian's *Fingal*. Luath Press was established in 1981 in the heart of Burns country, and is now based a few steps up the road from Burns' first lodgings on Edinburgh's Royal Mile.

Luath offers you distinctive writing with a hint of unexpected pleasures.

Most bookshops in the UK, the US, Canada, Australia, New Zealand and parts of Europe either carry our books in stock or can order them for you. To order direct from us, please send a £sterling cheque, postal order, international money order or your credit card details (number, address of cardholder and expiry date) to us at the address below. Please add post and packing as follows: UK – £1.00 per delivery address; overseas surface mail – £2.50 per delivery address; overseas airmail – £3.50 for the first book to each delivery address, plus £1.00 for each additional book by airmail to the same address. If your order is a gift, we will happily enclose your card or message at no extra charge.

Luath Press Limited

543/2 Castlehill
The Royal Mile
Edinburgh EH1 2ND
Scotland

Telephone: 0131 225 4326 (24 hours)
email: sales@luath.co.uk
Website: www.luath.co.uk